5

Aelbert Cuyp,
*The Mariakerk in Utrecht
viewed from the northeast.*
Black chalk, brown wash,
watercoloured in yellow
and red, 220 x 310 mm.
The British Museum, London

6

Aelbert Cuyp, *Utrecht
with the Vecht River and the
Pellekussenpoort.* Black chalk,
grey wash, watercoloured in
green, traces of pen in grey,
176 x 307 mm.
Staatliche Museen zu
Berlin-Preussischer
Kulturbesitz,
Kupferstichkabinett, Berlin

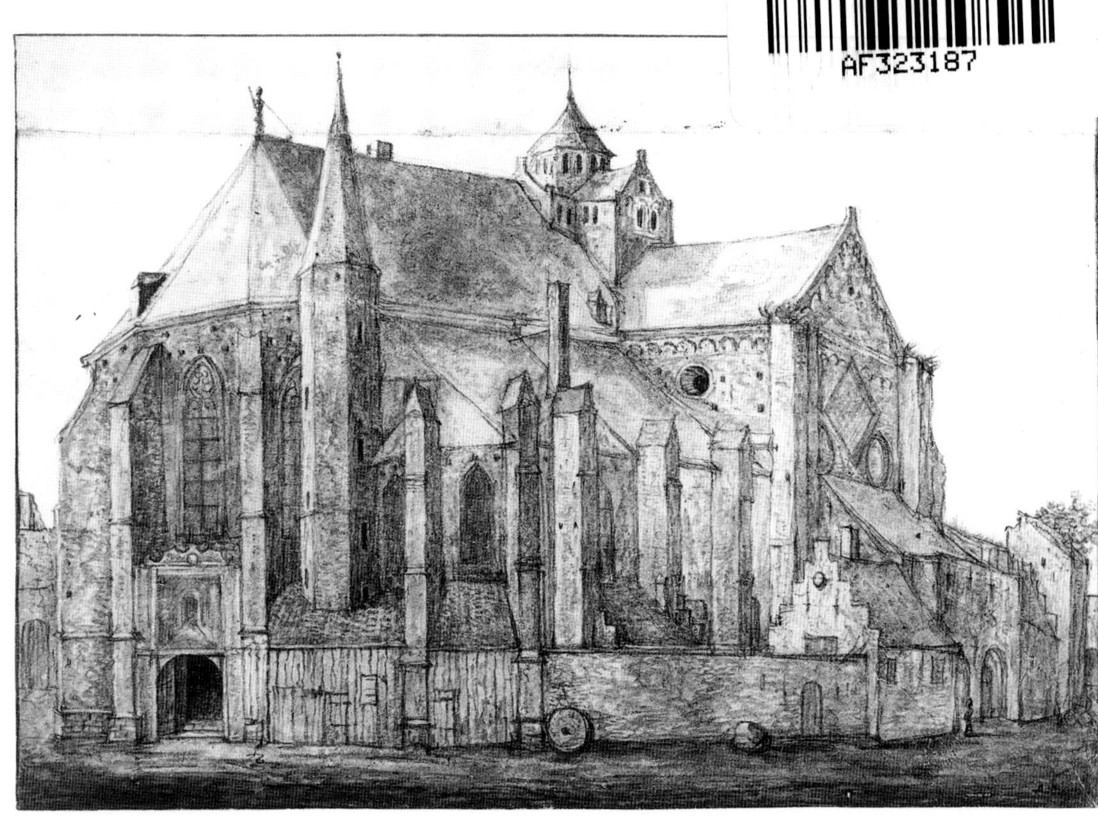

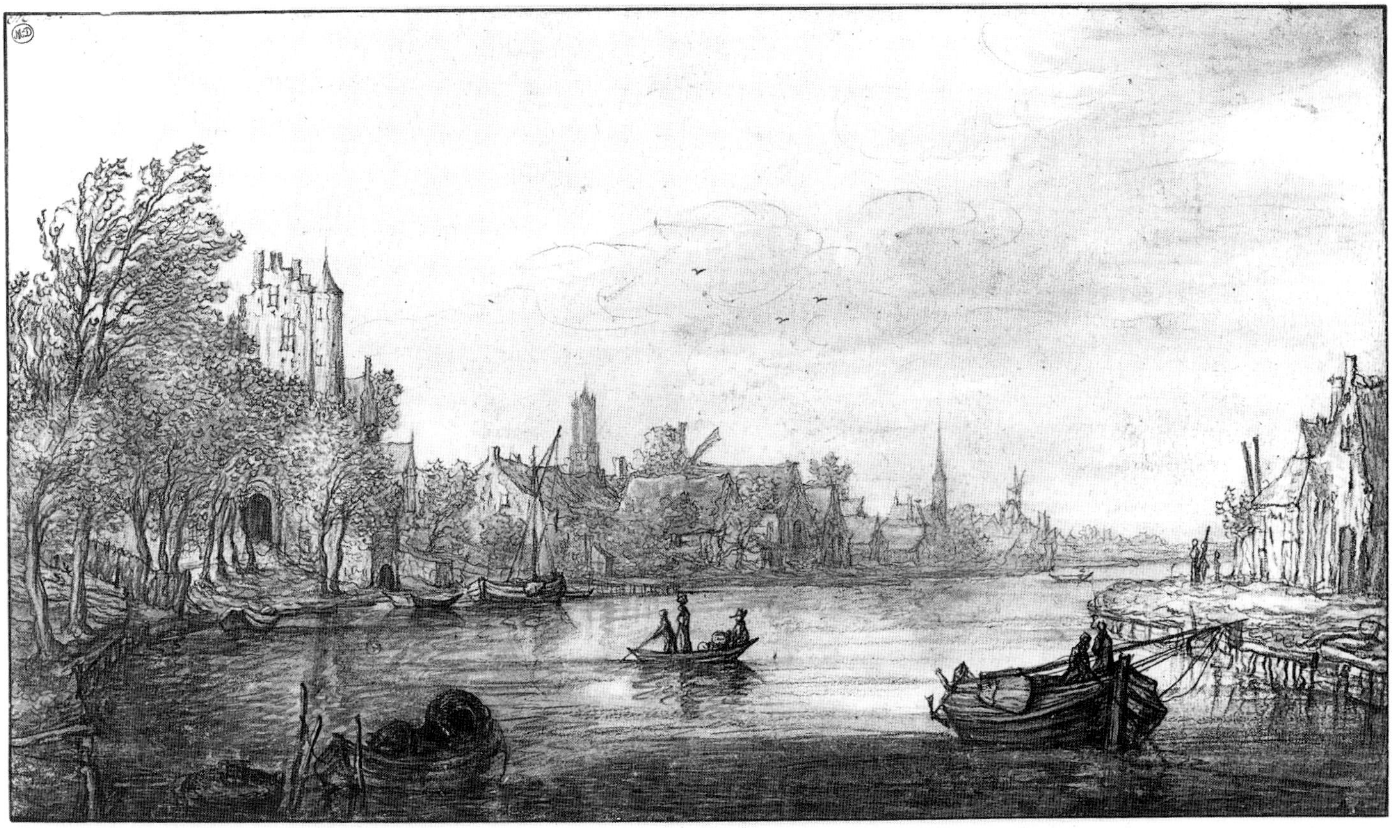

3

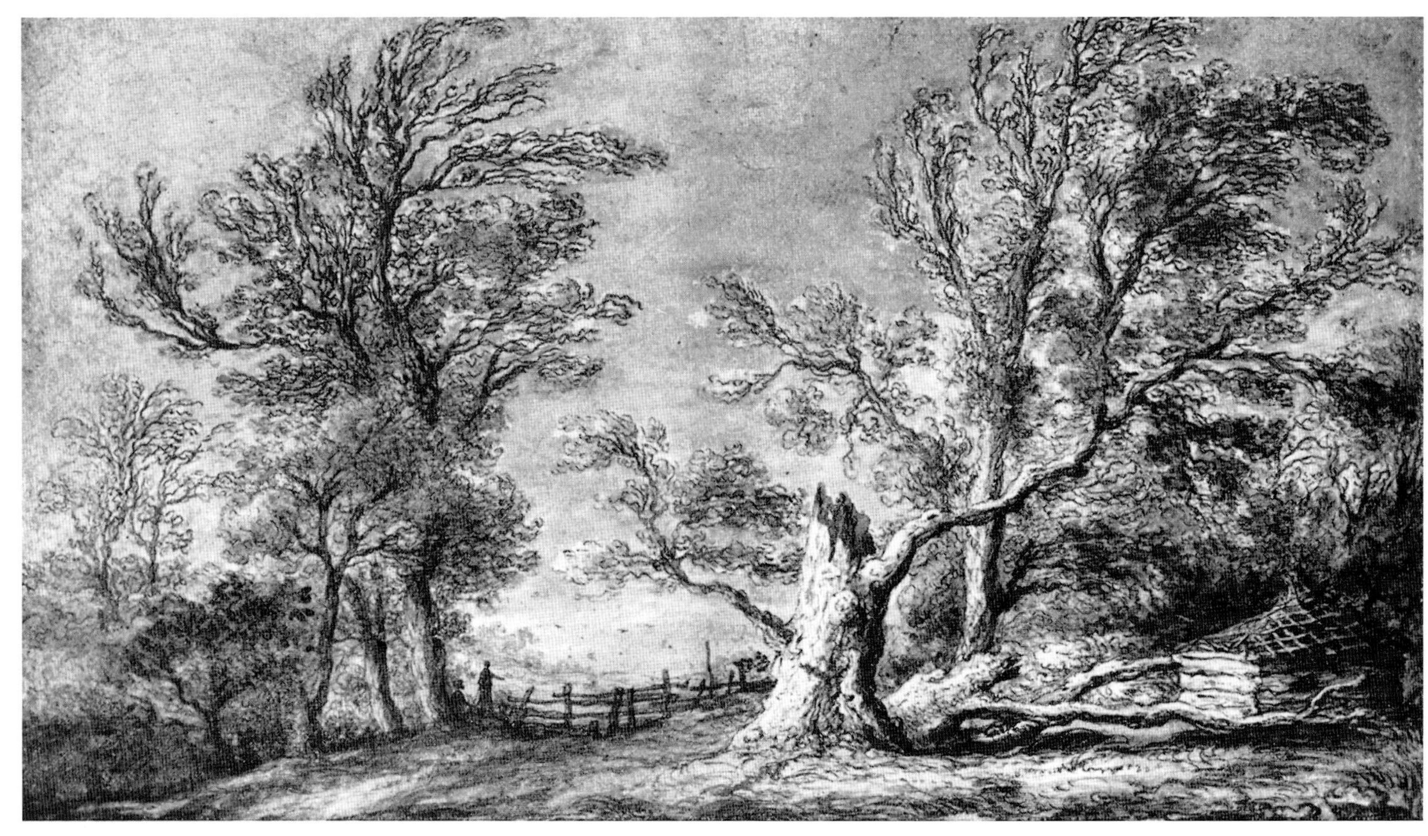

4

7

Aelbert Cuyp, *Landscape with old oak trees.*
Black chalk, grey wash, watercoloured, 193 x 310 mm.
Formerly Brower Collection, Pella, Iowa

like the *Landscape with old oak trees* (fig. 7), were undoubtedly made on a trip into the countryside to the east of Utrecht.

The young draughtsman soon overcame his uncertainty, as we can see from his *Utrecht with the Vecht River and the Pellekussenpoort* (fig. 6). In this drawing, which must have been made in or before 1639, he documents with great panache the rural character of the city, with the insignificant buildings outside the walls and with an inconsequential human presence – peasants crossing the Vecht. He laid down the drawing in chalk with a sensitive and at the same time accurate hand, and added shadows in grey wash. Then, perhaps in the studio later on, he enhanced the work with subtly applied colours. It seems likely that during this period Cuyp was seeking to identify his greatest strength. From his detailed drawing of *The Mariakerk in Utrecht viewed from the northeast* (fig. 5), it would appear that he was also exploring his potential as a specialist in architectural drawing at this time. Ultimately he decided on landscape drawing, his true talent.

Working eagerly, Cuyp built up a stock of drawings of subjects that he could use in paintings. We can see just how creatively he was able to employ these subjects from the relationship between one of his early paintings and several drawings. He based his *Cattle and herders, with the Mariakerk, Utrecht* (fig. 8) on a landscape sketch (fig. 7). In the drawing Cuyp made studies of a stricken oak tree, a dilapidated hut and a view through a fence with trees on either side. In the painting, the clumps of trees are spaced further apart to leave room for a much broader vista and for two herdsmen resting with their cattle. For the vista, Cuyp also used a drawing of the Mariakerk in

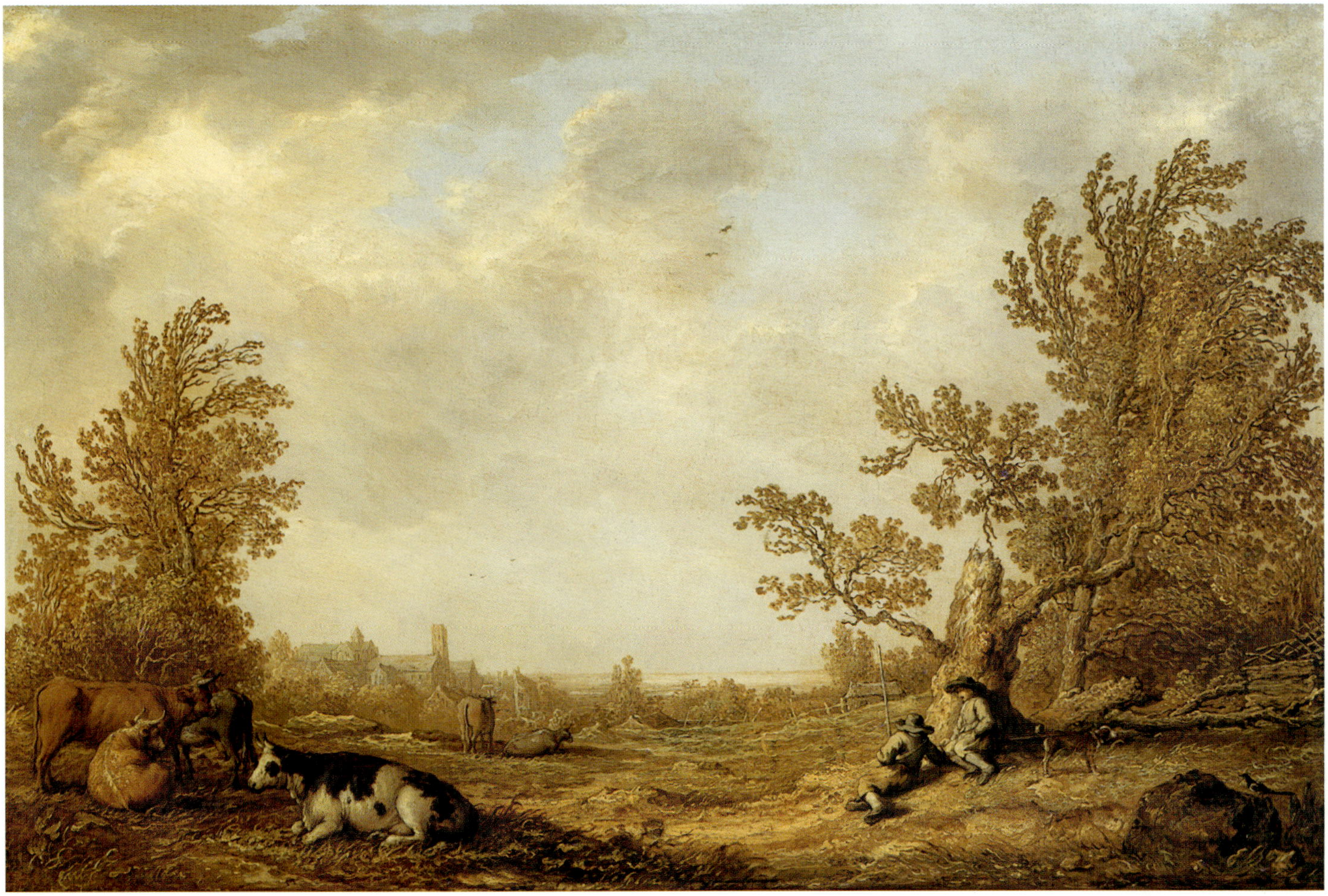

Utrecht, lifted out of its urban setting and used in silhouette against the sky, on the lower slopes of a ridge. The young Cuyp had some difficulty making space for vistas – that space which, in combination with the golden light, was to become so important in his later work. In the drawing, the view is confined to a glimpse between the clumps of trees. In the painting Cuyp needed the space for the herdsmen and their animals, which originally also included a horse – a horse that the artist overpainted with landscape and that can still just be made out on the right in front of the panorama. Cuyp must have realized that this horse was blocking the view that the herdsmen, and the viewer, can enjoy.

Cuyp's lightning-fast development around 1640 is evident in his *River view with dunes* (fig. 14), a drawing that was made only a year or two after the landscape with two clumps of trees (fig. 7). Cuyp took a bold approach when he sketched both the empty foreground and the distant expanse of this river view, which is probably in the area of the major rivers in Gelderland.

8

Aelbert Cuyp, *Cattle and herders, with the Mariakerk, Utrecht*. Panel, 49 x 74 cm. Residenzgalerie, Salzburg

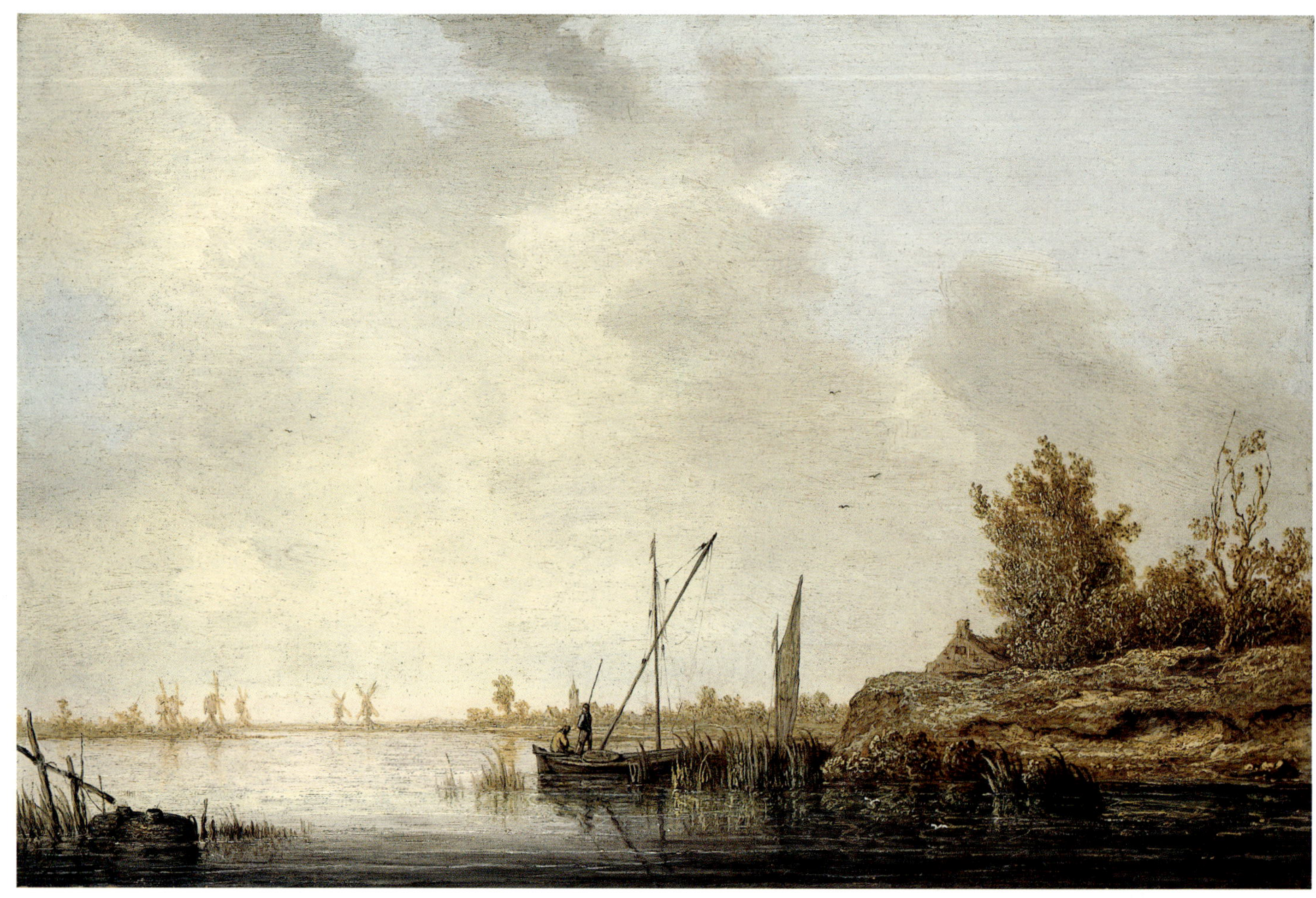

9
Aelbert Cuyp, *A River scene with distant windmills*.
Panel, 35.6 x 52.4 cm. The National Gallery, London

AROUND DORDRECHT

It was not a lack of subjects in his own surroundings that led Aelbert Cuyp to seek
and find inspiration in Utrecht, in the
woodlands and in the rolling landscape of
the great rivers. Cuyp recorded Dordrecht,
his birthplace, in numerous drawings and
paintings, and made many drawings in the
low-lying countryside outside the town.
A few small sheets, measuring some 15 by
20 cm, undoubtedly came from a sketchbook that he carried with him on his excur-
sions around Dordrecht, in which he made

usually very faithful studies from nature.
These sensitive drawings bear witness to
Cuyp's great love for his own familiar surroundings. In one of them (fig. 2) he recorded a pier on a windless afternoon with
extraordinary subtlety. The boats, still
rigged, have been pulled ashore between
the trees, while a single sailing vessel drifts
slowly away into the distance. Two cows
have walked into the water. Cuyp gave
colour to the work with delicate shading.
Although this and other drawings from
the same sketchbook give the impression

of being finished works, intended for the
market, Cuyp usually made use of these
sketches in his paintings. As a rule he did
not conceive of the drawings as a ready-
made plan for a painting, but rather took
elements from them. This method is nicely
illustrated by his *Windmills at Kinderdijk*
(fig. 10) and the associated panel (fig. 9).
It is clear from the fact that there is a view
of Dordrecht on the back that this drawing
did indeed come from a sketchbook. The
windmills at Kinderdijk occupy a prominent position on the left of the drawing,

while on the right the eye is drawn by a peasant cart on the dyke, fishermen and a farmer by a woven bank reinforcement. The most important place, however, is given to the tower of the church of Alblasserdam in the distance. Cuyp used large parts of this drawing in the painting, calling on another sketch for the boats and the fishermen in the centre. The anecdotal details on the right have disappeared and the human presence is confined here to the two fishermen, who have been placed, with great audacity, right in front of the church tower in the distance. The figures are no more than minimal accents compared with the vast expanse of sky.

The album was not devoted solely to landscapes. Occasionally Cuyp sought to combine landscape elements with cattle and plants, as in the drawing of some cows on a dyke with vegetation, probably butter-bur (fig. 11). Sometimes he studied the plants at the water's edge in detail (fig. 12). Studies like this also served him in his paintings, both in his early years and later. Other drawings are studies of cattle or domestic animals, among them a dog that he portrayed with great feeling for the texture of the short coat (fig. 13).

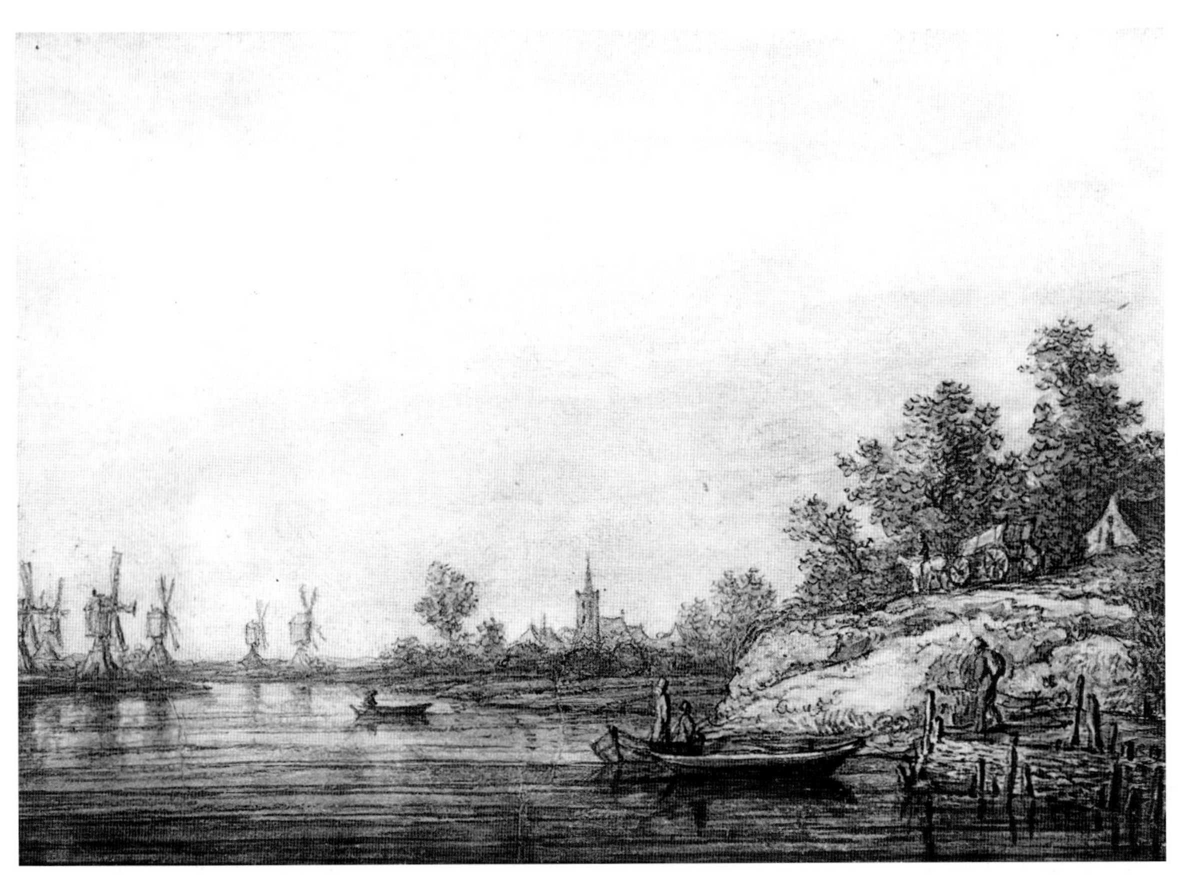

10

Aelbert Cuyp, *Windmills at Kinderdijk*.

Black chalk, grey wash,

watercoloured in brown and red,

137 x 189 mm. Private collection, USA

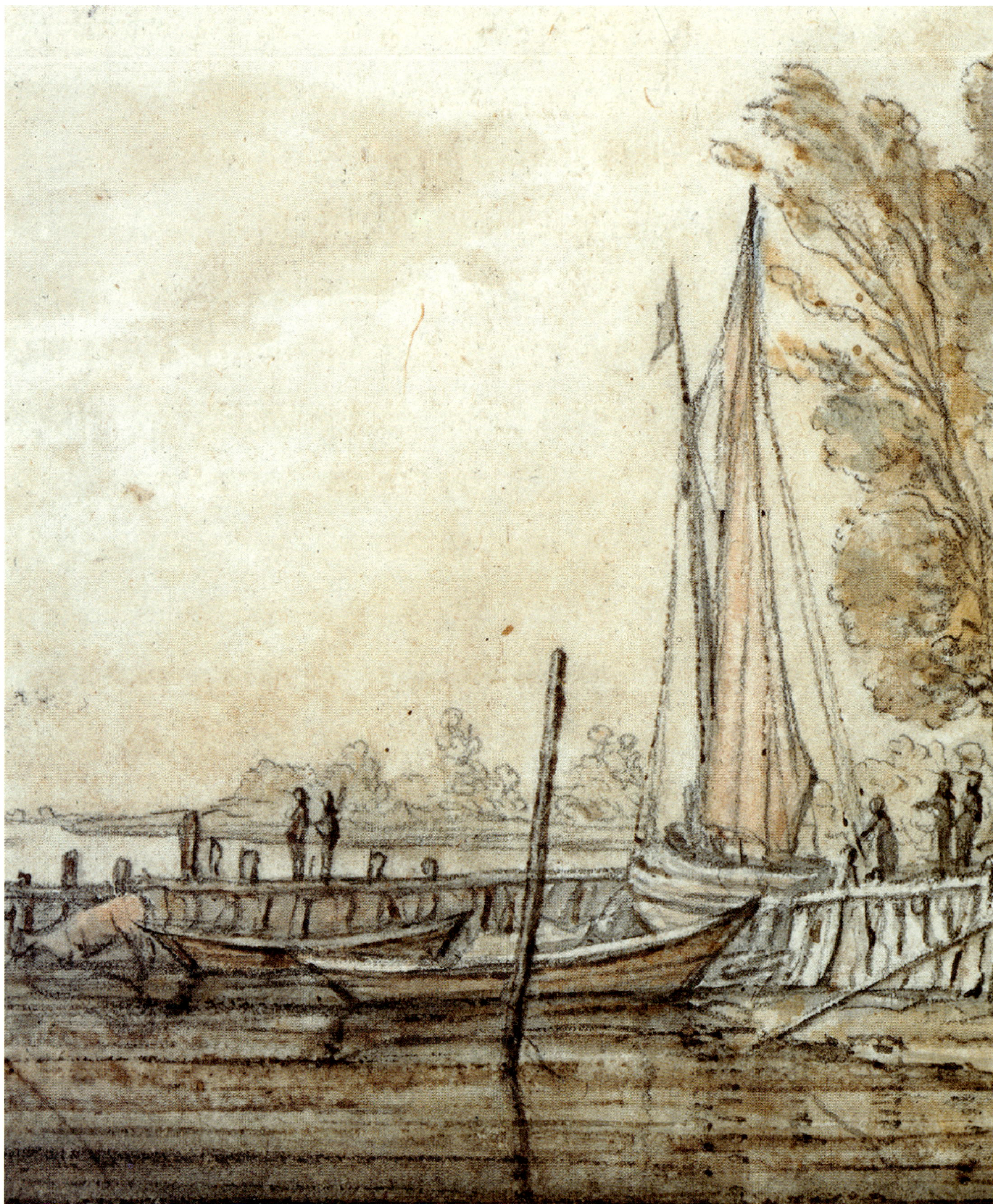

8

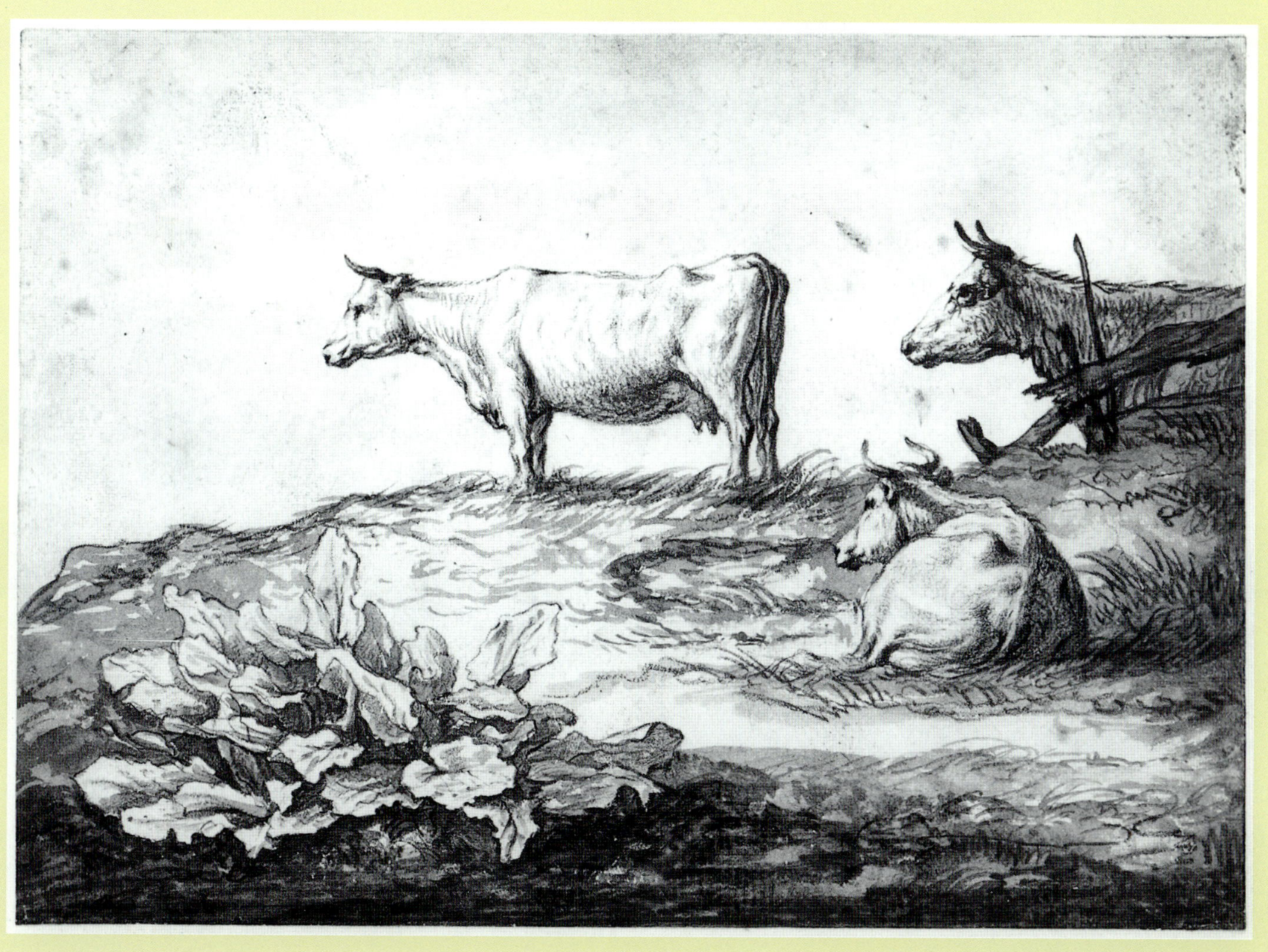

11

Aelbert Cuyp, *Three cows near a fence with
butterbur in the foreground*. Black chalk, grey wash,
watercoloured in brown, yellow and red,
heightened with white, 140 x 190 mm.

The British Museum, London

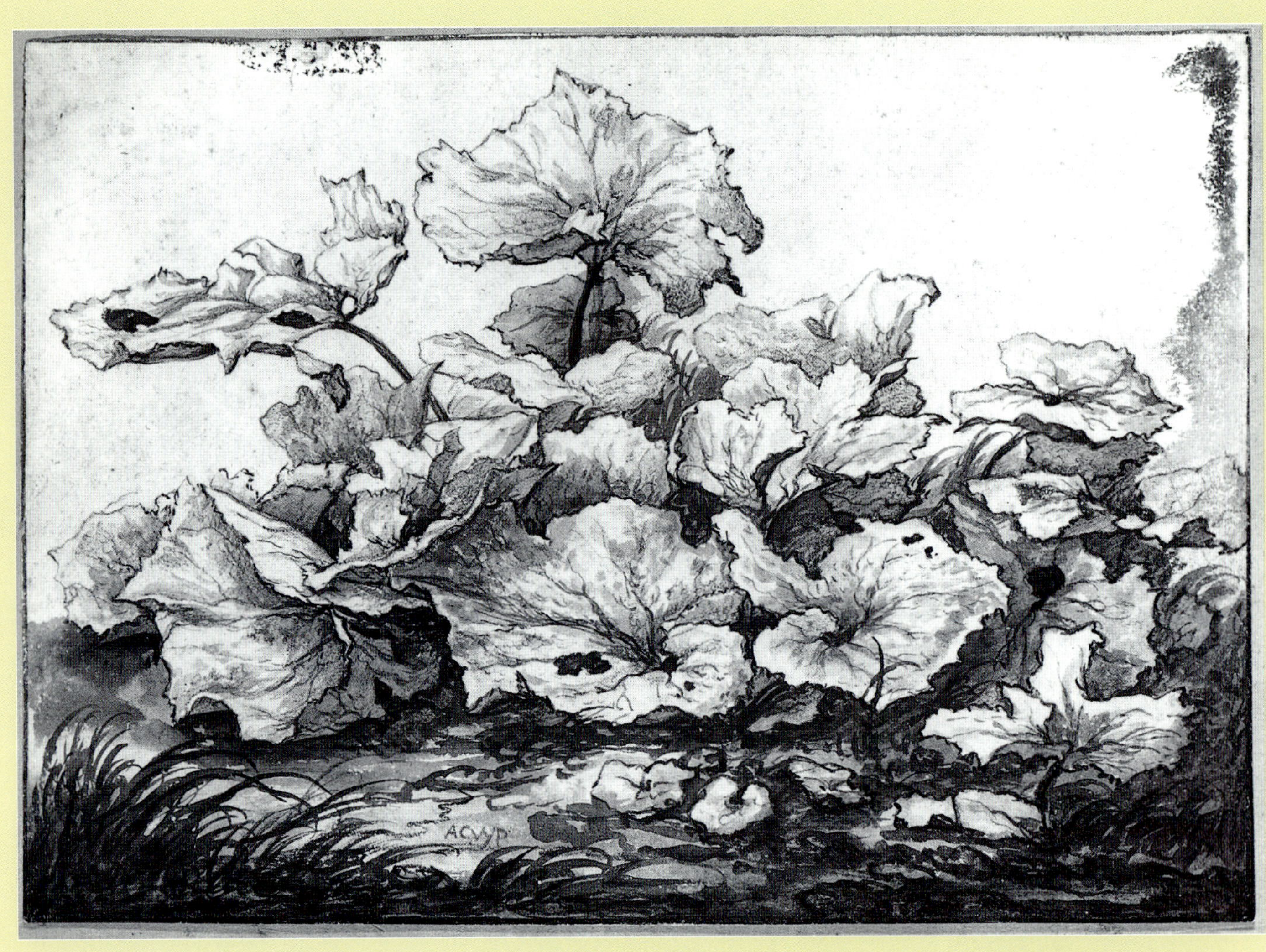

12

Aelbert Cuyp, *A Study of plants, possibly butterbur.*
Black chalk, grey wash, watercoloured in
green and yellow, 140 x 194 mm.
Collection Frits Lugt, Institut Néerlandais, Paris

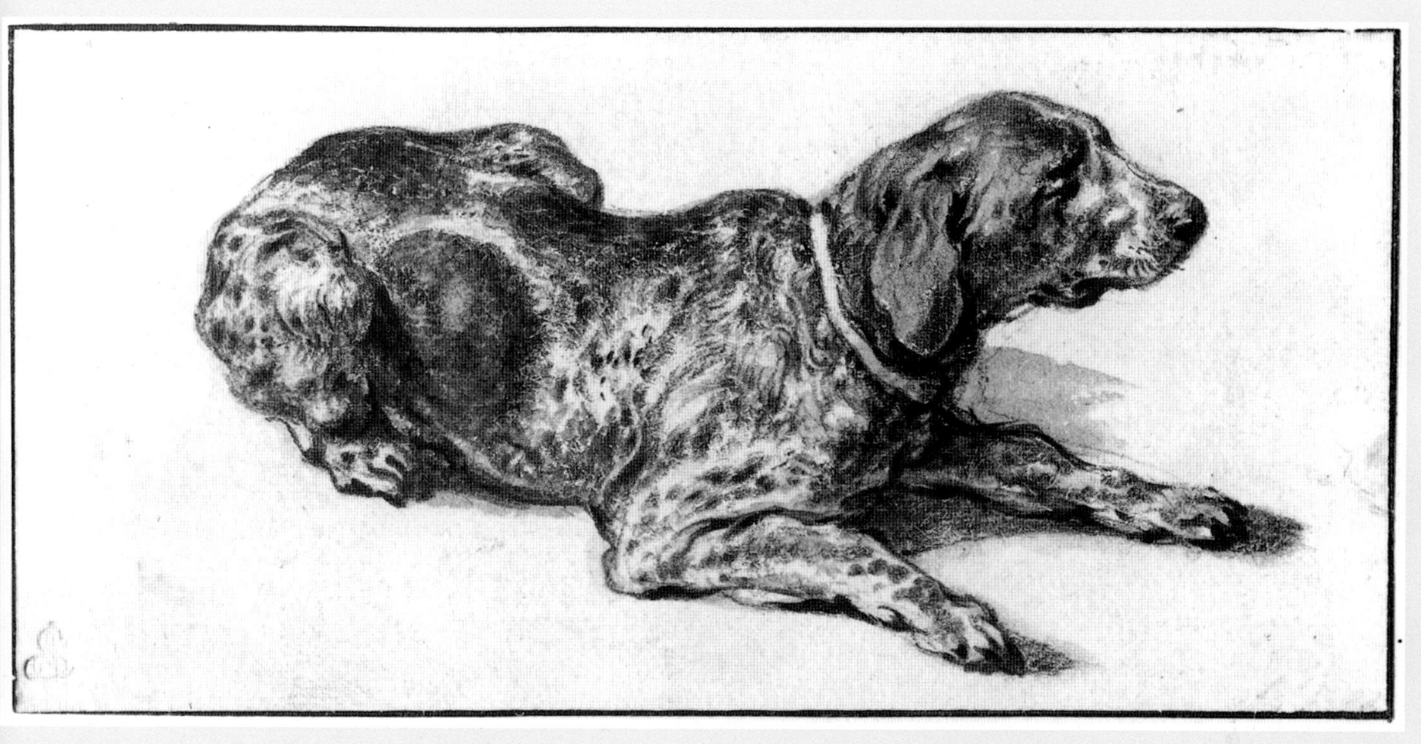

13
Aelbert Cuyp, *A dog lying down.*
Black chalk, grey wash, watercoloured in
brown and green, 71 x 143 mm.
Graphische Sammlung Albertina, Vienna

Several powerful, wide drawings of panoramas are the high point of Cuyp's drawn oeuvre. Most of them are views of towns and cities, but there are also purely landscape vistas, among them his *River view with dunes* (fig. 14), which he must have made shortly after 1640. During this period Cuyp travelled in Holland, to The Hague, Scheveningen, Leiden, Rijnsburg and Haarlem. He also went east, to the Rhine valley near Cleves and Kalkar. We do not know whether he went on one grand tour or went on several trips, nor whether he went east first and then to the Dutch cities or vice versa. The drawing (fig. 14) was probably made along one of the great rivers, possibly in the area around Cleves. It reveals astonishing control of the emptiness of the foreground coupled with a magnificent, suggestive distance, a landscape that invites the viewer to explore what is around the next bend. At the same time, the supple routine that emerges from the views of Arnhem, Harderwijk and Leiden (figs. 16-18) is still lacking here.

Cuyp probably sketched the drawings swiftly during the trip and worked them up with colour when he returned home. Darker areas were brushed with gum arabic – which makes the dark passages glossy and deep black – and this may well also have been done later. The reason why the views of Arnhem and Harderwijk resemble each other may be that Cuyp drew the two places on one of his trips in the Veluwe or through the Gelderland valley. It is, however, also possible that he happened to work up the two drawings in the same way once he got home. The fine, strong working of the trees is similar to that in his early paintings, like *Cattle and herders, with the Mariakerk, Utrecht* (fig. 8). In *The Hague viewed from the northwest* (fig. 15), the skyline of the city is little more than a ragged line on the horizon, behind bare dunes without much texture, convincingly modelled and strikingly watercoloured in yellow and green. He

12

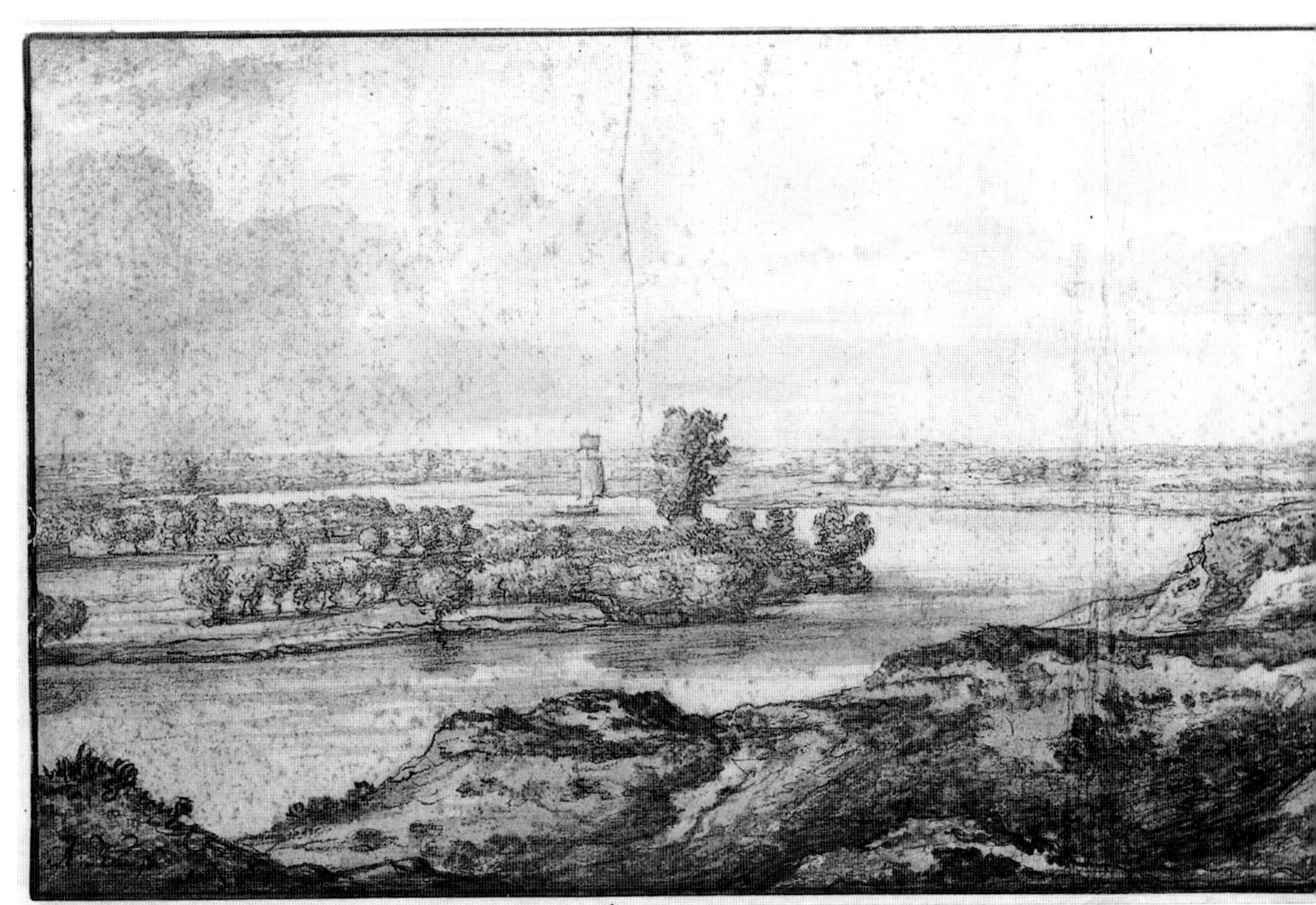

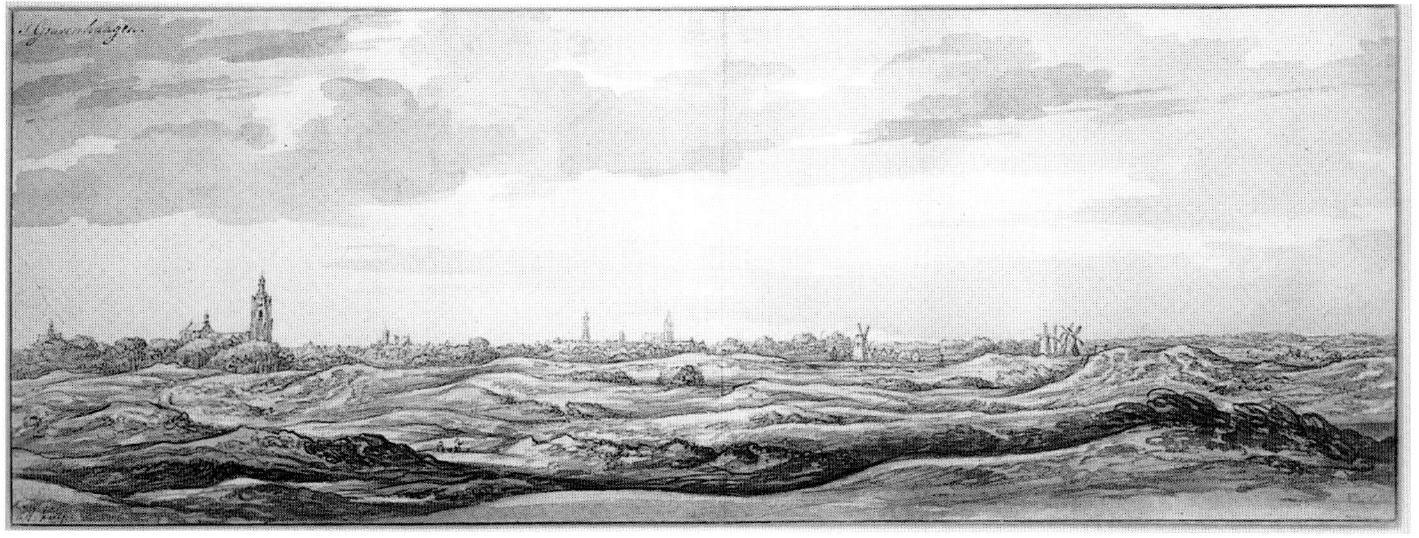

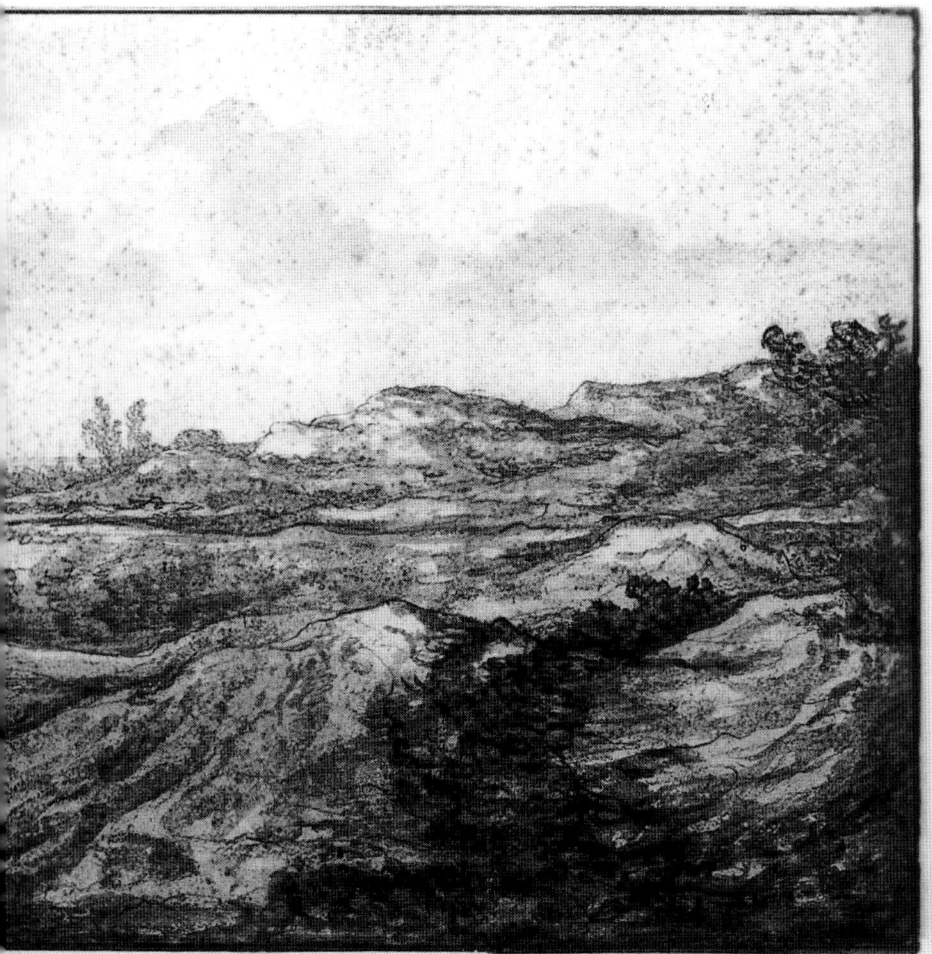

15 ∧
Aelbert Cuyp, *The Hague viewed from the northwest.*
Black chalk, grey wash, watercoloured
in yellow, red and brown, 185 x 494 mm.
Rijksmuseum, Amsterdam

14
Aelbert Cuyp, *River view with dunes.*
Black chalk, grey wash, watercoloured,
185 x 480 mm. Rijksmuseum, Amsterdam

summed up Leiden, too, in a wide drawing
(fig. 18) – here again the foreground dominates, now however with a bend in a road
by a rivulet with a long fringe of reeds. And
finally Cuyp immortalized Dordrecht in a
number of panoramas, of which *Dordrecht
viewed from the east* (fig. 19) most closely
resembles the sheets he drew on his travels.
Here again, Cuyp achieves a wonderful
interplay of water, reeds and a distant city.

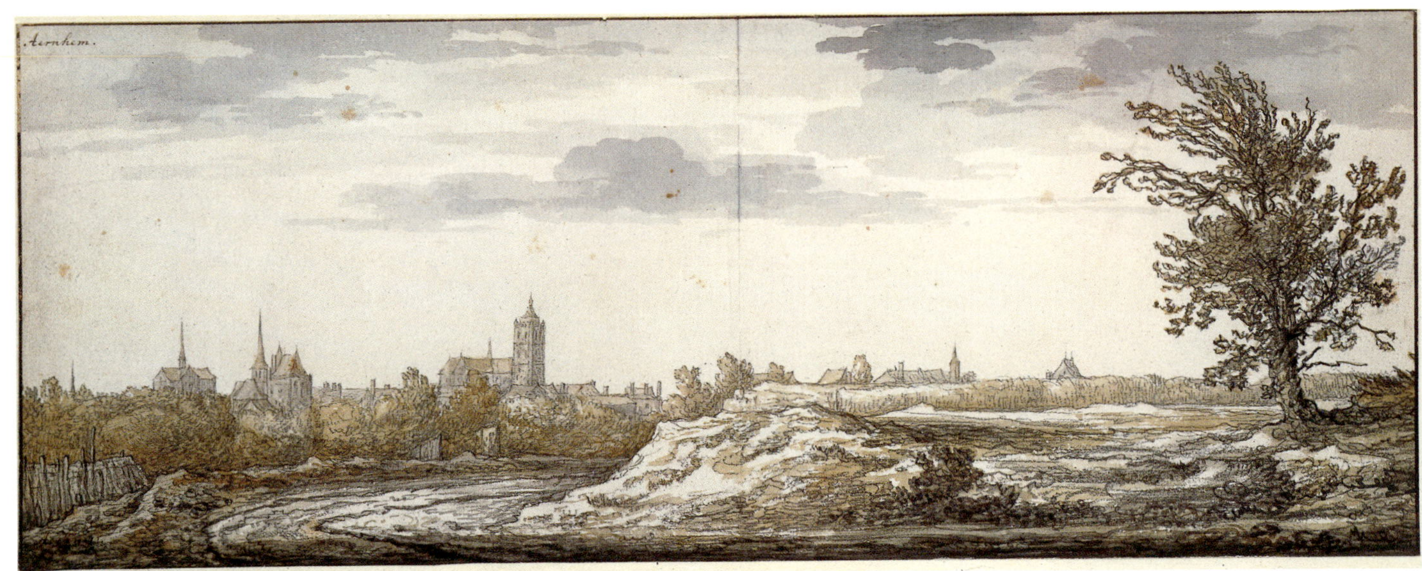

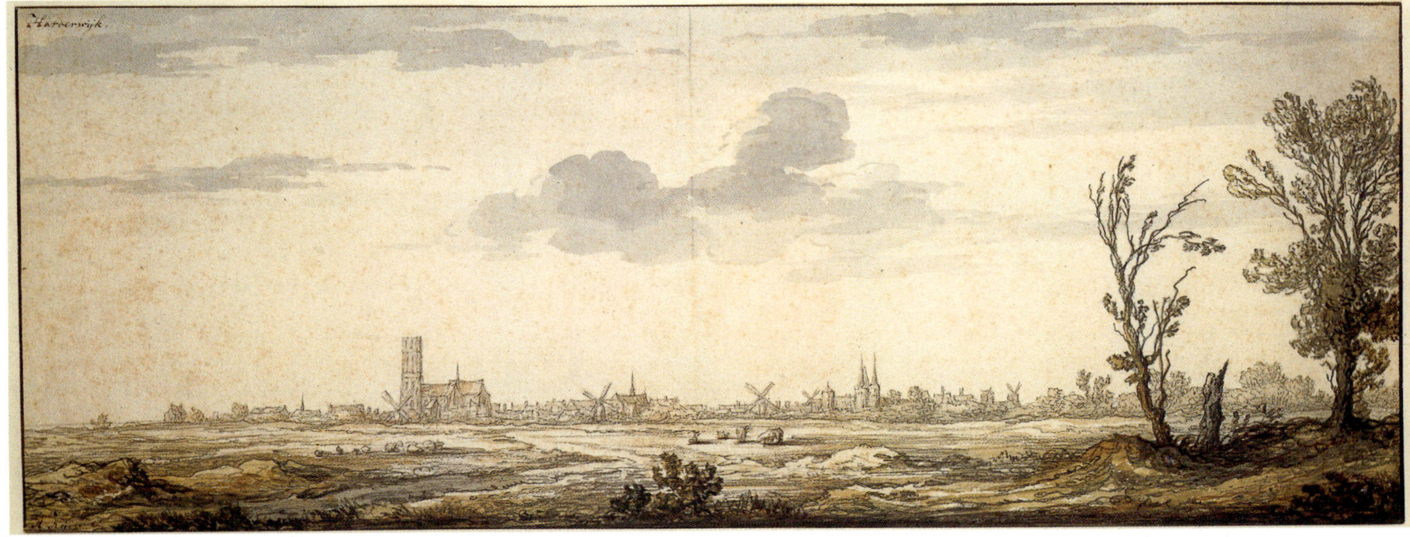

16

Aelbert Cuyp, *Arnhem viewed from the northwest.*
Black chalk, grey wash, watercoloured in yellow and
green, 190 x 486 mm. Rijksmuseum, Amsterdam

17

Aelbert Cuyp, *View of Harderwijk.*
Black chalk, grey wash, watercoloured in brown and
green, 185 x 433 mm. Rijksmuseum, Amsterdam

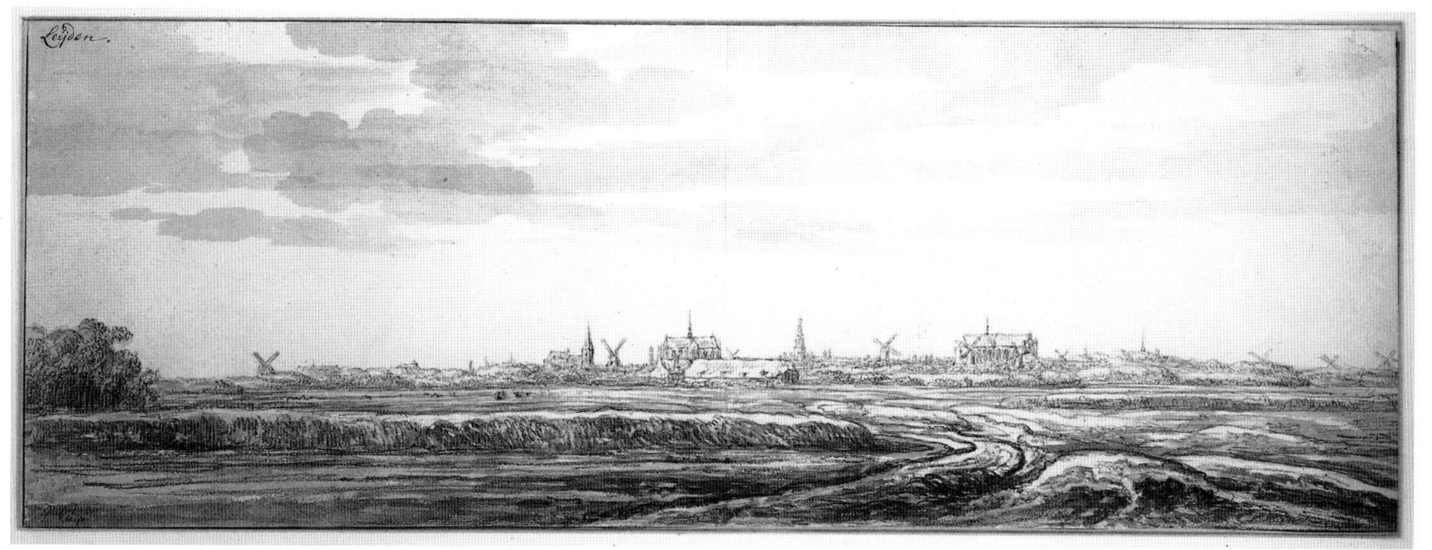

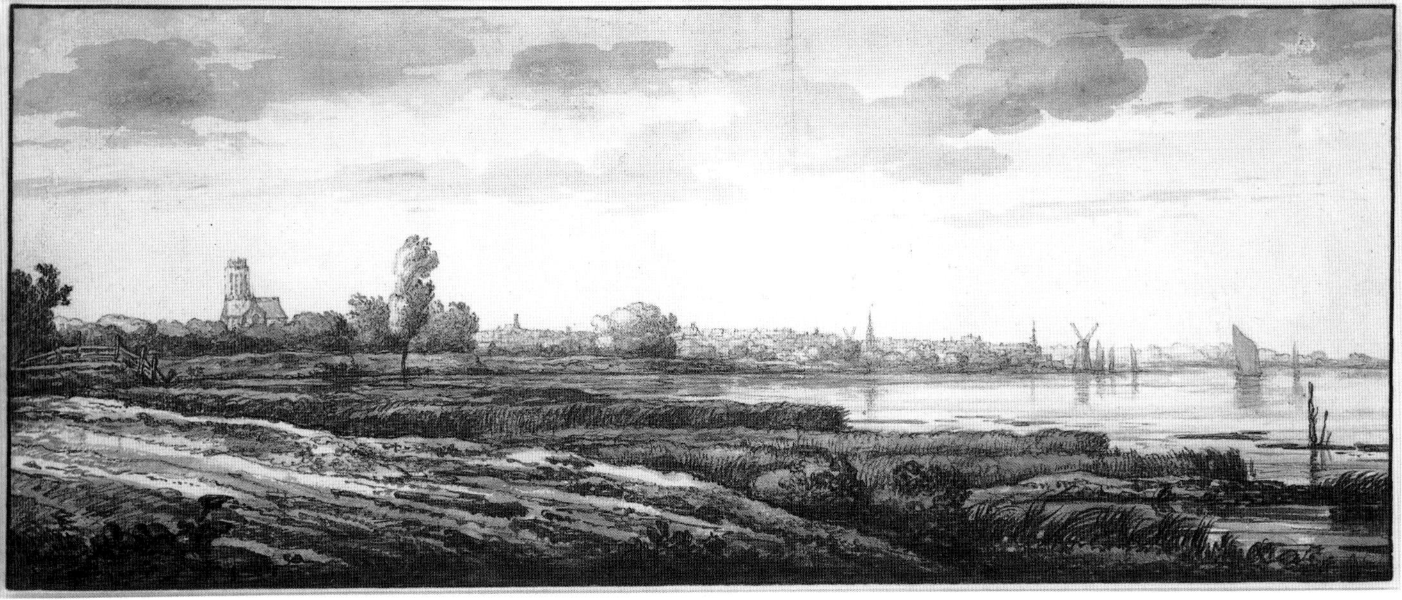

15

18

Aelbert Cuyp, *View of Leiden*.

Black chalk, grey wash, 187 x 497 mm.

Rijksmuseum, Amsterdam

19

Aelbert Cuyp, *Dordrecht viewed from the east*.

Black chalk, grey wash, watercoloured

in brown and green, 190 x 445 mm.

Rijksmuseum, Amsterdam

Aelbert Cuyp undoubtedly had his first art lessons from his father, Jacob Gerritsz Cuyp (1594-1652). The ambitions of Cuyp senior, who has an eclectic mix of scenes from the Bible, still lifes, market scenes and portraits to his name, must have been considerable. However, popular in Dordrecht primarily as a portrait painter, he never achieved more than local fame. Jacob, in turn, was the son of the stained glass artist Gerrit Gerritsz Cuyp (c. 1565-1644), who also took on other work, including decorating the city's harpsichord in 1604. It was important to the young Aelbert's education that both his grandfather and his father took in pupils and had studios where artistic products of a certain standard were made. An inventory of goods owned by Aelbert's grandfather reveals that he had 'art books' and other illustrated works. This inventory was compiled in 1621, after the death of Jacob's mother. At that time Jacob was just embarking on his career, and he will undoubtedly have consulted these books on more than one occasion. Other members of the Cuyp family also worked as painters or stained glass artists. The best known of them is Jacob's half brother Benjamin Cuyp (1612-1652), who worked in Utrecht and The Hague as well as in Dordrecht. His extensive oeuvre of rapidly executed paintings (fig. 23) was of only incidental influence on his gifted nephew.

In his youth Jacob Cuyp worked in Abraham Bloemaert's studio. The influence of this Utrecht master can be discerned in a number of Jacob's paintings, and it is also evident that he had looked at works by Gerard van Honthorst, Hendrick Bloemaert and Jan van Bijlert. In a large painting (fig. 21) a seated young woman, the embodiment of Dutch prosperity, is depicted in a landscape with a little boy who shows the viewer a bunch of buttercups. Jacob later developed the motif of figures in a landscape in portrait groups of families or of children on their own, enjoying the outdoor life in the company of animals. Paintings like this, along with standard portraits (fig. 22), were Jacob's speciality. Later in his career Aelbert was to tackle the same genre in his own way (fig. 44).

In Utrecht, Jacob Cuyp met Aertken Cornelis van Koothendochter, the woman he was to marry in 1618. It seems likely that Jacob later sent his son Aelbert to the city to learn the more refined tricks of the trade. The drawings that Aelbert made in Utrecht around 1640 (figs. 5, 6) prove that he spent some time there, although there is not a single written record of the visit. It is, however, clear that Aelbert was significantly influenced by landscape artists who came from Utrecht or who had ties with the city – men like Roelant Saverij, Herman Saftleven and Jan Both. It should be noted here, however, that Saverij died in 1639 and did very little in his last few years. Cuyp could also have met Gorinchem-born Herman Saftleven in Rotterdam, where the latter's brother Cornelis worked. Cornelis was another artist who almost certainly influenced Cuyp. Evident contact between Herman Saftleven and Jan Both in Utrecht in the early 1640s, however, makes it likely that Cuyp encountered these artists there. We cannot rule out the possibility that Cuyp studied in Rotterdam. Simon de Vlieger, who remained in Rotterdam until 1652 and was a good art teacher, appears to have had an influence on Cuyp's landscapes and marine paintings. It is also not impossible that at some point Aelbert watched Jan van Goyen (1595-1656) at work. His numerous journeys certainly took Van Goyen to Dordrecht, while Aelbert Cuyp in his turn visited The Hague in the early 1640s. Van Goyen's love of panoramas with a view of a city (fig. 20) may have helped Aelbert to make his own choices (fig. 16). It is moreover precisely those drawings that Cuyp made in the vicinity of The Hague and Haarlem which betray Van Goyen's influence.

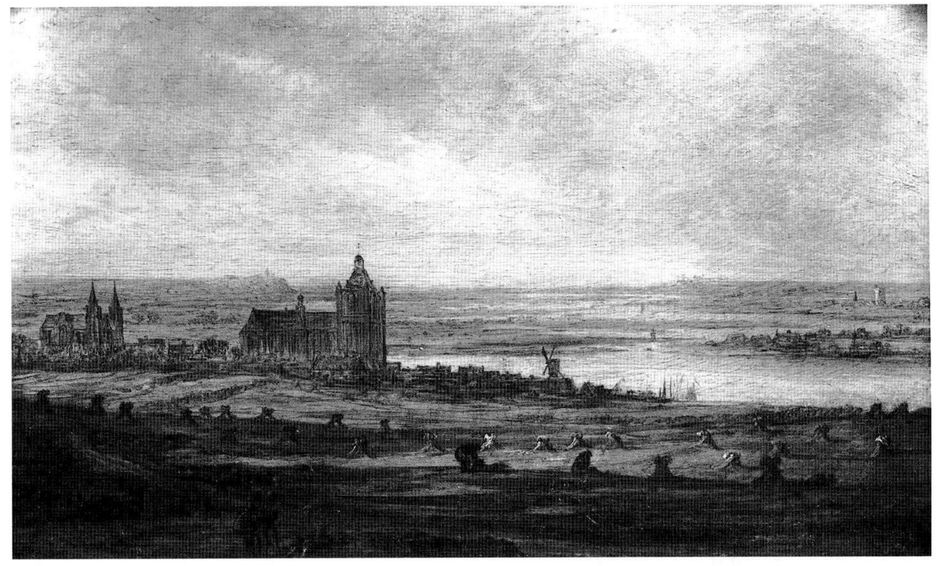

20

Jan van Goyen, *View of Arnhem*.

Panel, 26 x 41.5 cm.

Rijksmuseum, Amsterdam

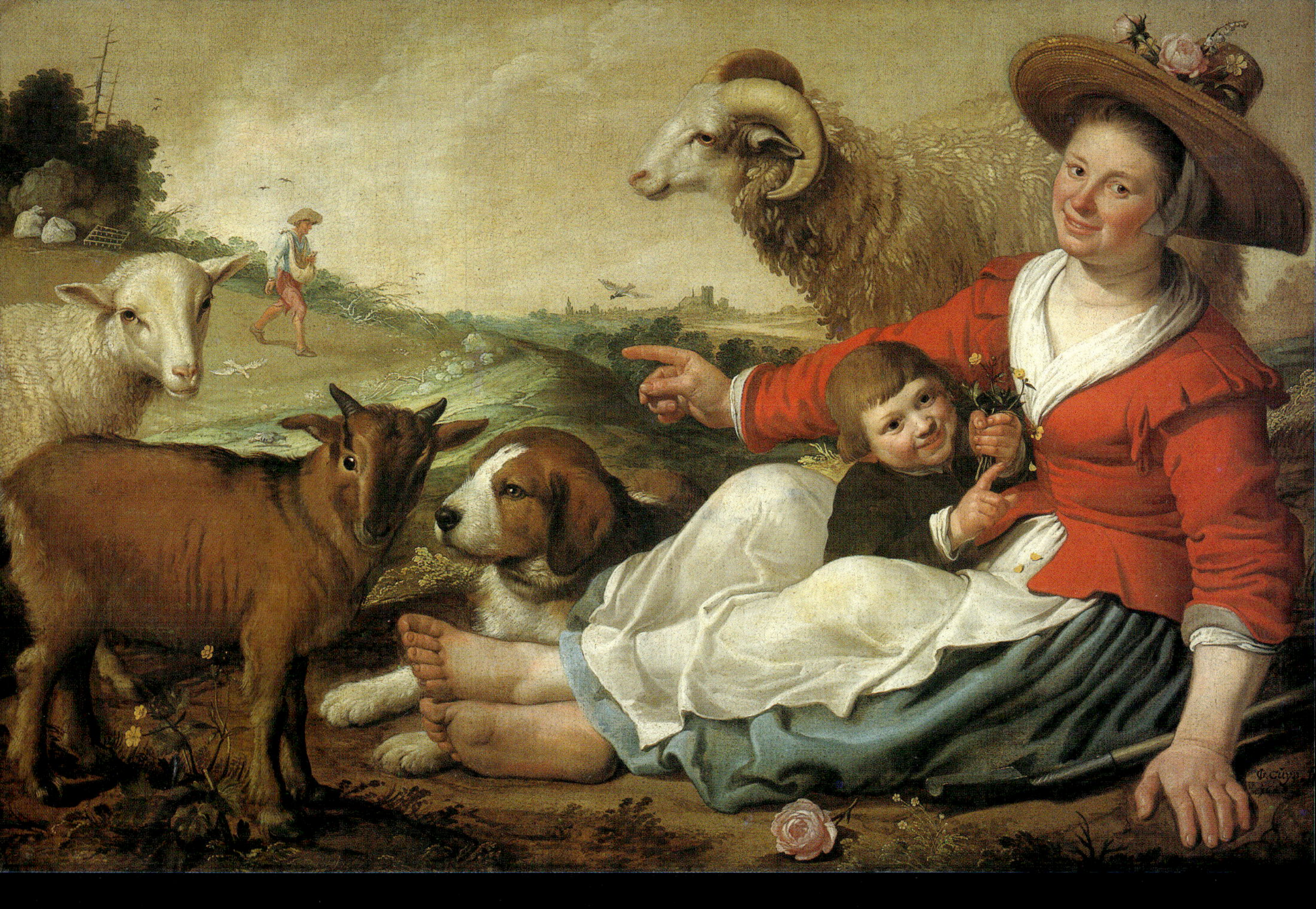

21

Jacob Gerritsz Cuyp, *The shepherdess*, 1626.

Canvas, 122 x 168 cm.

Rijksmuseum, Amsterdam

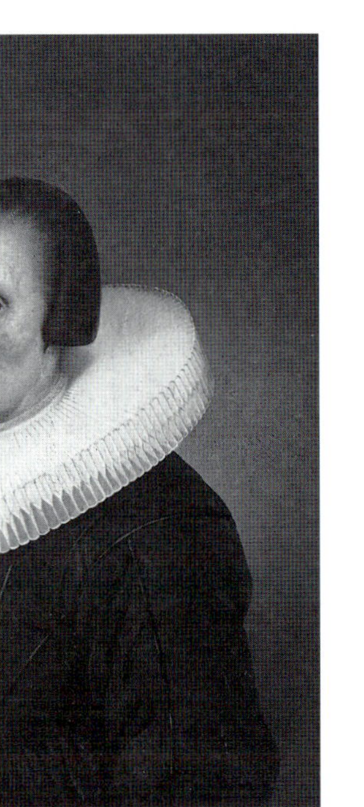

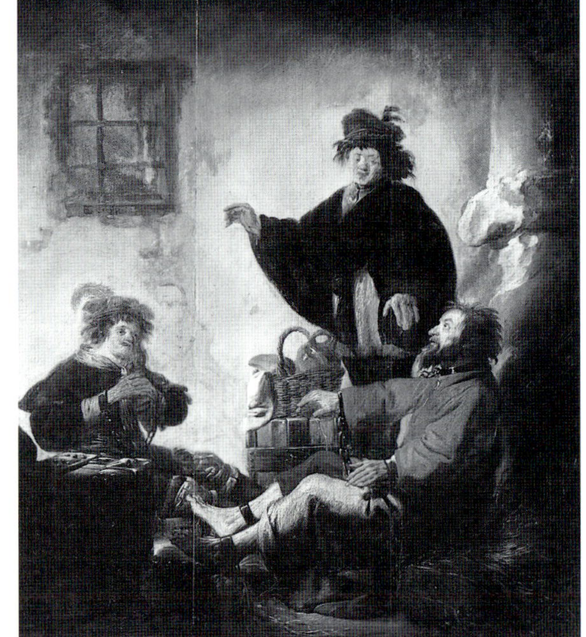

22

Jacob Gerritsz Cuyp,
Margaretha de Geer, 1651.
Panel, 74 x 59 cm.
Rijksmuseum,
Amsterdam

23

Benjamin Cuyp,
Joseph interpreting the dreams
of the baker and the butler.
Panel, 73.5 x 62 cm.
Rijksmuseum,
Amsterdam

18

Around 1640 the artistic environment in
Dordrecht had little to offer. Strangely
enough, the city is however the birthplace
of a number of important Dutch painters,
some of whom must have studied with
Jacob Cuyp. Broadly speaking, Aelbert
Cuyp has little in common with those
storming talents – Ferdinand Bol, Nicolaes
Maes, Samuel van Hoogstraten, Godfried
Schalcken and Aert de Gelder – most of
them painters who left Dordrecht in search
of a career. In Aelbert's oeuvre, generally
speaking, we can discern little influence of
Benjamin Cuyp (fig. 23) or of Rembrandt,
who took several pupils from Dordrecht
into his studio. The *Portrait of a man with a*

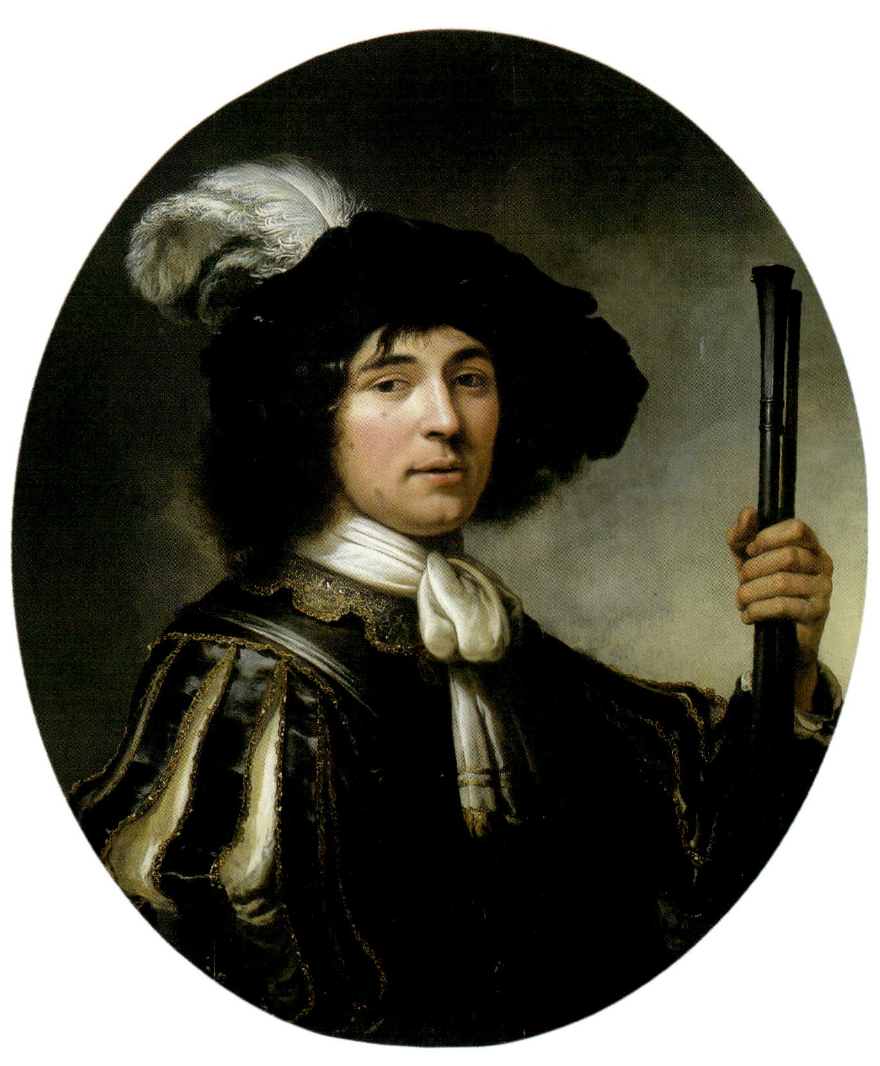

24

Aelbert Cuyp, *Portrait of a man with a rifle.*
Panel, 80.5 x 68.5 cm. Rijksmuseum, Amsterdam
(on loan from the City of Amsterdam,
A. van der Hoop bequest)

rifle (fig. 24) would, however, be almost inconceivable without a knowledge of Rembrandt's *tronies*.

Jacob Cuyp was a minor all-rounder, but Aelbert evidently preferred a career as a specialist. The great talent for landscape that Aelbert displayed in his drawings could be utilized in his father's work. Father and son worked together around 1640 on some portrait groups in a rural setting. They were signed by Jacob, but have a landscape background based on drawings by Aelbert or actually painted by him. The aim in the Cuyp studio was apparently to divide the work along traditional specialist lines – the father made the portraits and the son painted the landscape backgrounds. Very soon, however, Aelbert must have devoted himself exclusively to his own specialism.

Around the time of Jacob Cuyp's death in 1652, Aelbert painted several portraits that are almost indistinguishable from his father's work. Evidently Aelbert considered continuing his father's portrait business, which probably provided a fairly steady income. The *Portrait of a man with a rifle* (fig. 24) likewise dates from this period and illustrates Cuyp's best efforts in the field of portraiture – this time, however, according to a formula of his own without too many references to his father's work. The painting is unsigned but is almost certainly the pendant to a portrait of a woman which is signed, and is dated 1651 (fig. 25). The young man's head, with its full lips and the dark mole accentuating the red of the cheeks, has extraordinary vitality.

The solid position that Jacob Cuyp had acquired for himself in Dordrecht was Aelbert's springboard to social success. Jacob had an organizational role in the Walloon Church; he produced illustrations for the works of Jacob Cats, at that time the Pensionary of Dordrecht, and Johan van Beverwijck, physician and writer on health. In 1658 Aelbert married Cornelia Boschman, the widow of Johan van den Corput. Although he had not been without means before this, upon his marriage Aelbert became a wealthy man who moved in Dordrecht's leading circles. He became an elder of the Reformed Church, Regent of the Heilige Geest- en Pesthuis of the Grote Kerk and councillor of the High Court of South Holland. In the wills that he and his wife made, there are references to the paintings in their house and initially also to paintings yet to be made, but on his death he was referred to in his role as councillor, not as an artist. We may take it that his career as a painter rapidly took a back seat after his marriage.

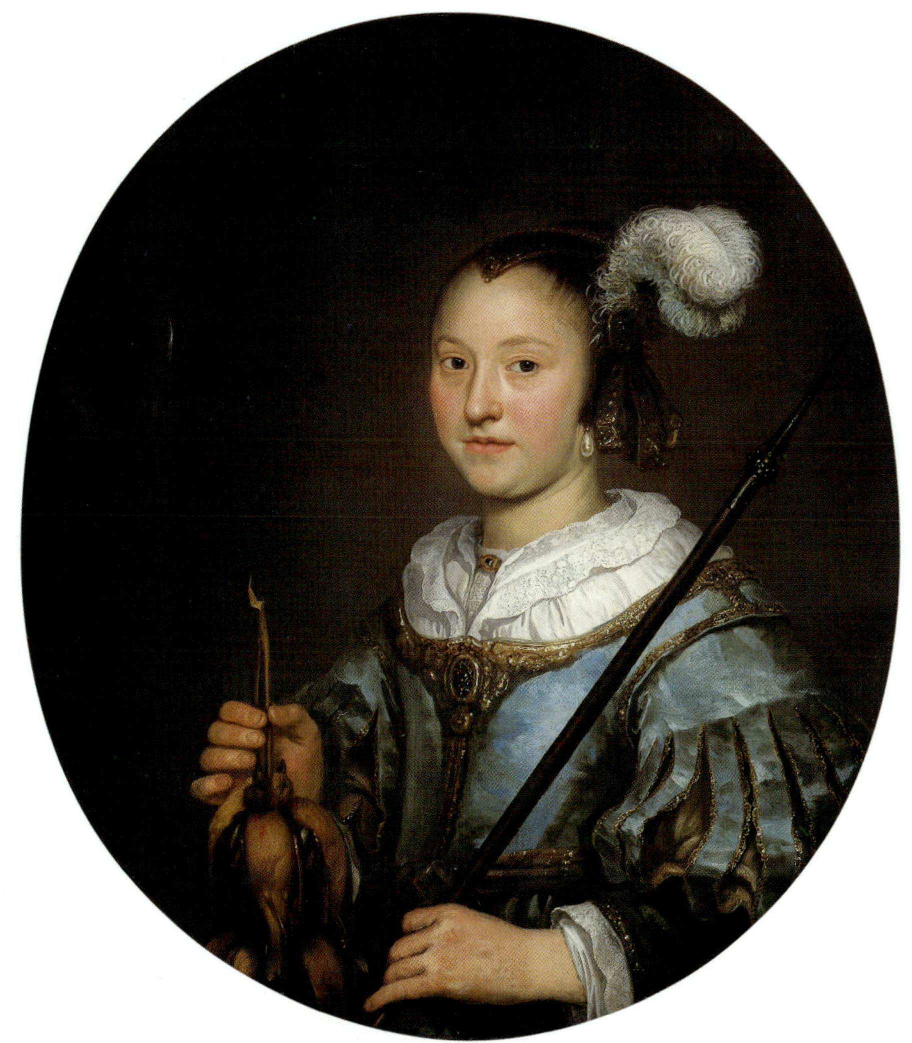

Aelbert Cuyp,

Portrait of a woman aged twenty-one as a hunter, 1651.

Panel, 80 x 68.5 cm. Private collection, USA

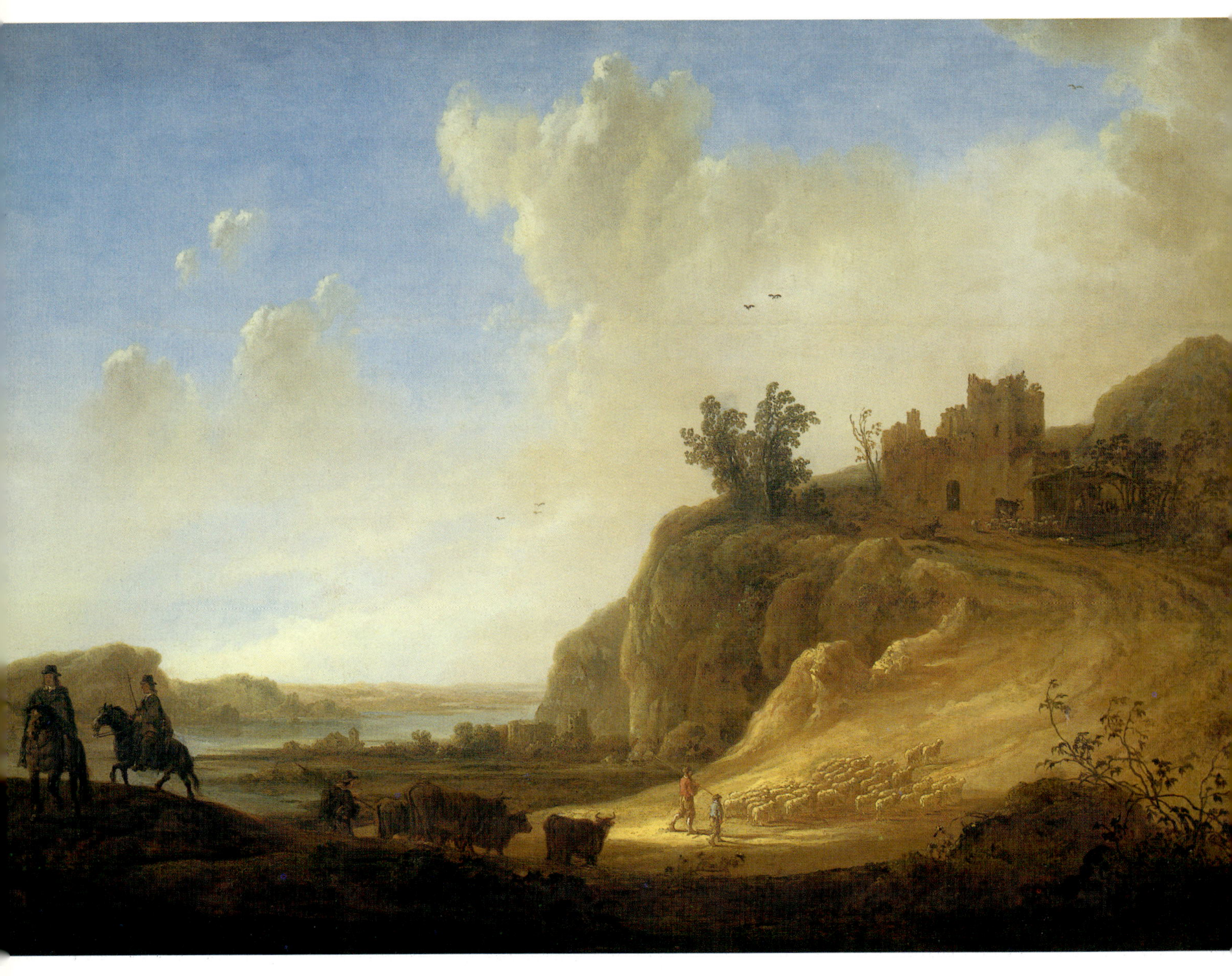

26

Aelbert Cuyp,

Mountainous landscape with the ruins of a castle.

Panel, 66.5 x 91 cm.

Rijksmuseum, Amsterdam

CONTRE-JOUR

In the 1640s Aelbert Cuyp discovered *contre-jour*. This is a French term – literally 'against the light' or 'into the light' – used to describe the effect of sunlight coming from just outside the pictorial plane, so that a yellow to pink glow floods the landscape from one side. In these paintings, the viewer feels that he would be able to see the sun if he could only look around the edge of the frame. The addition of long shadows suggests the light of the late afternoon. This manner of depicting light and sky – the clouds are often rendered in dramatic shades of gold and rose – perfectly reflects 17th-century artists' fascination with capturing the mood of the day. No longer was a landscape bathed in an even light, in which every element was given the same degree of attention – now the light in the painting made it possible to concentrate much more strongly on the most important areas.

Associated with this is the silhouette effect: the light falling from the side means that people, animals and trees can be reduced to shadow images and all the attention can be focused on what really matters in the landscape. Not infrequently there will be pointing figures, but there might also be a strong *repoussoir*. This is another French term, from the verb meaning 'to push back'. It is a means of achieving perspective by placing a large figure or object – a group of trees, for instance – in the foreground like a sort of scenic frame, drawing the viewer's eye into the painting and creating the illusion of depth.

Neither of these effects was discovered by Cuyp himself; they were developed by northern European painters working in Italy, by artists like Paul Bril, Adam Elsheimer and Claude Lorrain. We can only assume that friends of these artists returned to Holland with enthusiastic accounts and, using examples of their own work, demonstrated to their colleagues how to achieve these effects. What we know for certain is that in the Netherlands a whole school of painting came into being, with masters who specialized in Italian landscapes and warm sunlight – a group of artists who were later dubbed 'the Italianates'. Dutch painters will also undoubtedly have seen prints by these masters. The etching by Claude Lorrain (1600-1682) of the meeting between Eliezer and Rebecca (fig. 28), in which small figures cast long shadows and a herd moves slowly over a bridge, for example, could have made an impression on Cuyp. A brief stay in the Netherlands by Herman van Swanevelt (c. 1600-1655), who was in close contact with Claude, probably had a great deal to do with promoting the introduction of these artistic effects. In 1643 Swanevelt spent a short time in Woerden, the town where he was born, on his way from Rome to Paris, where he was to become court painter. A painting signed by him in Woerden in 1643 or 1648 (fig. 27) might be an important document in dating the introduction of Italianate art in the Netherlands. And artists like Cornelis van Poelenburch, Bartholomeus Breenbergh and Jan Both also appeared in the Netherlands at or around this time with similar works. Aelbert Cuyp may have seen the work of these artists in Utrecht.

Cuyp used these effects in a highly individual manner, both in paintings with an unmistakably Dutch character and in images of an imaginary foreign country. One example of the latter category is

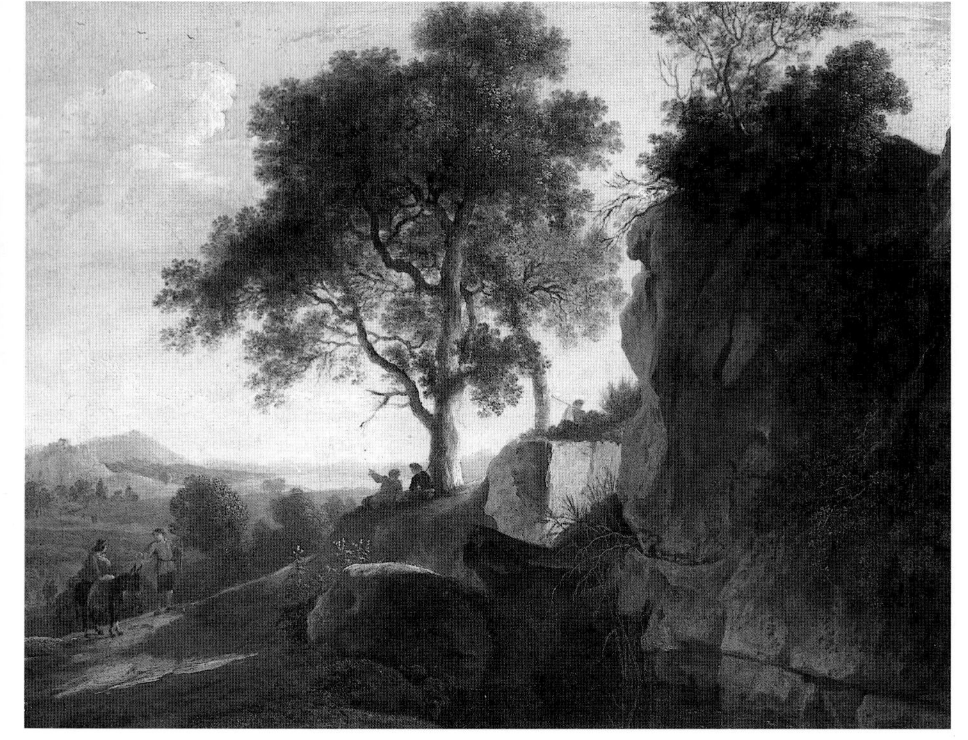

27

Herman van Swanevelt, *Italian landscape*,
1643 or 1648. Canvas, 56 x 69 cm.
Rijksmuseum, Amsterdam

Claude Lorrain, *The meeting of Eliezer and Rebecca.*

Etching, 128 x 194 mm. Rijksmuseum, Amsterdam

Mountainous landscape with the ruins of a castle (fig. 26). It is very evident from this painting that Cuyp had never been further than the area of the Lower Rhine around Cleves and had never seen real mountains. Nevertheless, it would not be fair to dismiss this work as a cardboard mountain landscape. There is a splendid tension between the two riders climbing a peak on the left and the two flocks being driven by shepherds to the right, up the hill towards a barn beside a ruined castle. A river in the low-lying land between the mountains leads the eye past the ruins of a second castle and a village to a hazy prospect. Delicate blue, yellow, pink and white colour the cloudy sky with light entering from the left, a palette interspersed in the landscape with gentle brown and grey-green shades.

Whereas the Italianate artists used these effects primarily for paintings with exotic subjects, Cuyp also used them for Dutch landscapes, as he does in his *Cows by the water* (fig. 29). This painting, like the *Mountainous landscape with the ruins of a castle*, must have been painted in the mid 1640s. The colours are similar to the palette used in that painting, particularly the browns and greyish greens. The sky on the left is yellow, in a comparable *contre-jour*. The atmosphere here is somewhat ominous, as if thunder might rumble at any moment. The cows stand out in silhouette and their calm placidity suggests that the tension in the muggy air leaves them completely unmoved. Quite soon after this Cuyp returned to the subject of cows by a river in several other paintings, where he depicted them in strong, clear colours (fig. 30). The comparison with similar paintings with their crystal clear light and the not entirely pristine condition of *Cows by the water* have meant that there has been little interest in this painting in the last few decades. It must, however, have been one of the first times that Aelbert Cuyp concentrated, in a painting, on cattle in the grand manner in his own Dutch setting.

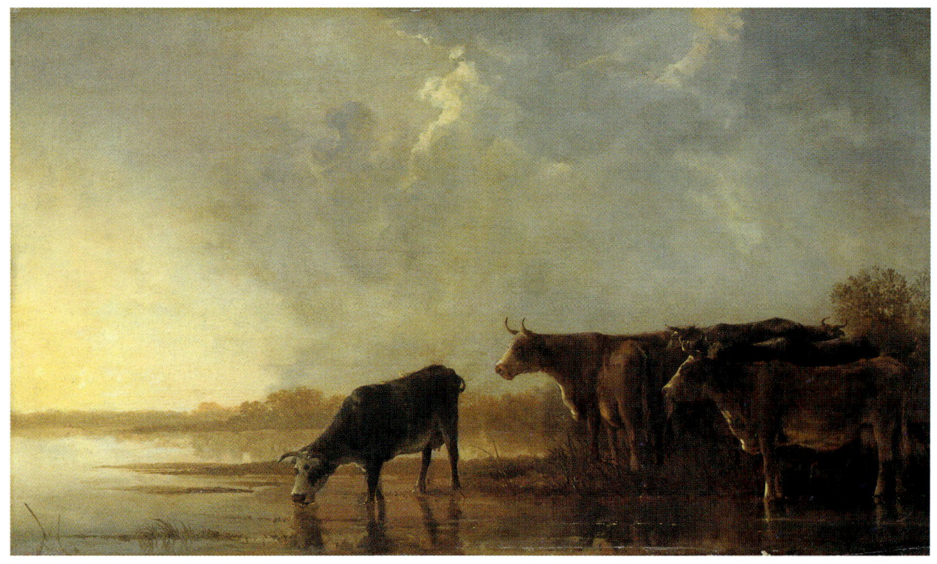

Aelbert Cuyp, *Cows by the water.*

Panel, 42.5 x 72 cm.

Rijksmuseum, Amsterdam

COWS

Aelbert Cuyp was a masterly painter of cows. His fame in this field is such that virtually any anonymous drawing and every unsigned 17th-century painting of cows has been attributed to him at one time or another. Cuyp's great strength was that he was able to capture so tellingly the placid calm that cows can radiate, as in the sketch he made around 1650 (fig. 55). He achieved this fine result after constant study. A comparison with the *Three cows near a fence with butterbur in the foreground* (fig. 11) from the early sketchbook tells us that the artist must have studied cows time and time again. Before this, Aelbert also used animal studies by his father. A series of engravings by Reinier à Persijn (fig. 31) after drawings by Jacob Cuyp, published in 1641, is certainly based on old material that Cuyp senior had had lying around since the 1620s. The young Aelbert was, as we can see from his earliest paintings, not averse to borrowing from these animal studies, which may have been part of his father's studio 'stock'. The cow lying down and viewed from the back, on the left in his painting in Salzburg (fig. 8), was made after an example by his father. In his diligent studies, Aelbert Cuyp revealed himself to be an exemplary pupil, who painstakingly took the steps of the *aemulatio*, the competition with older artists: he followed his father's example, tried to equal it in the London drawing (fig. 11), and surpassed it in his later drawing (fig. 55).

Cuyp used different methods in order to achieve this. In his *Cow lying and cow standing* (fig. 32) he used minimal lines and a light wash in grey ink for the shadows. In his *Studies of a cow and a horse* (fig. 56) he used different techniques for the two animals. For the cow he tried to convey the animal's bulk with parallel lines placed inside the outline with the tip of a moist brush. The horse, too, is contained within an outline, but here Cuyp has succeeded in defining the animal with a broad brush in darker ink. In the cow the emphasis is on the folds of the skin, particularly around the neck; in the horse the focus is on light and shade.

Probably shortly after 1650, Aelbert worked up a number of his own sketches into a series of etchings (figs. 33-35) whose small format (they are shown here actual size) and sensitive use of line lend them immense charm. In two of them (figs. 33, 34) we find cows which, on a larger scale, can be seen in *A cow lying and a cow standing* (fig. 32). The drawing may perhaps have come from Cuyp's stock of drawn examples. The animals in the etching are reversed, of course, as a result of the printing process. In another etching (fig. 35) Aelbert gives us five cows in a minimal landscape, one behind the other in an almost swinging harmony. It is a trifling little etching of a trifling subject, and yet it is so natural and touching.

23

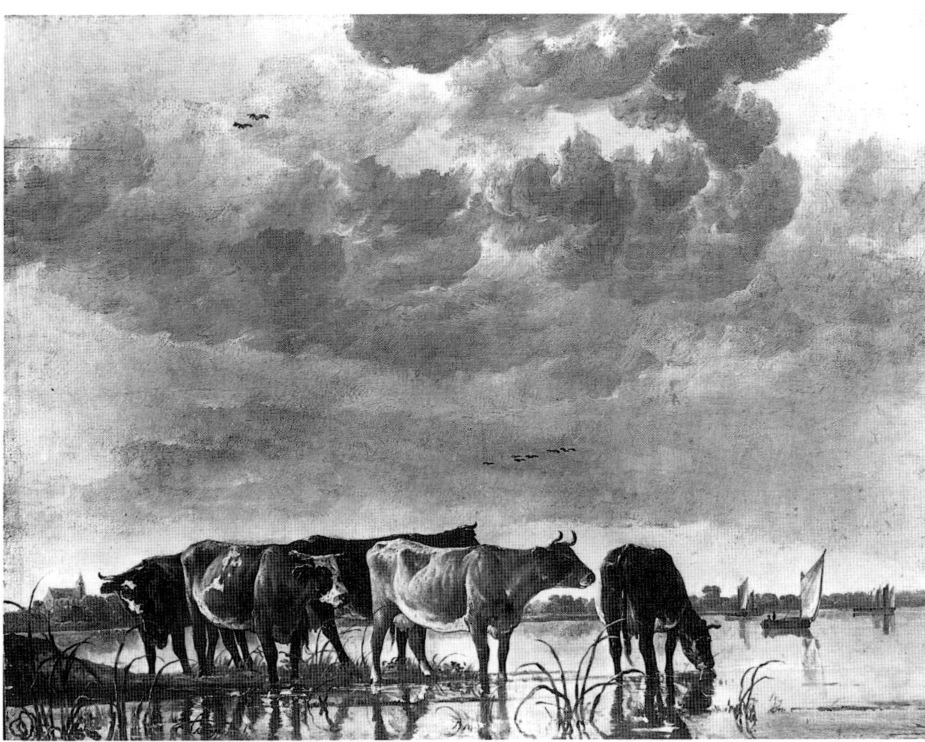

30

Aelbert Cuyp,
Cows in a river.
Panel, 59 x 74 cm.
Szépmüvészeti Múzeum,
Budapest

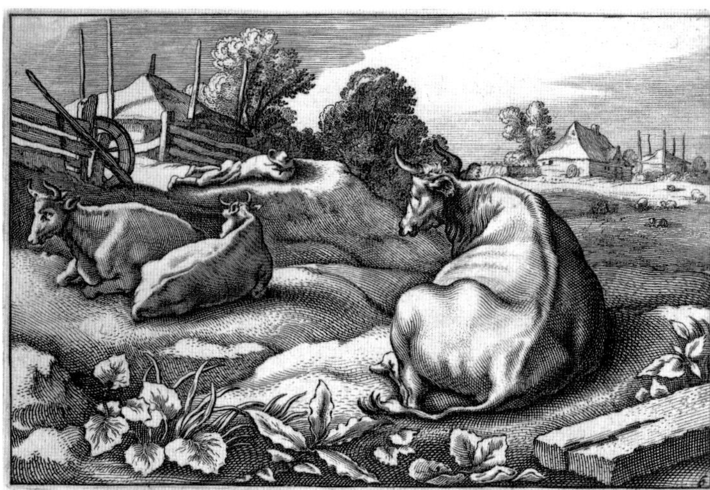

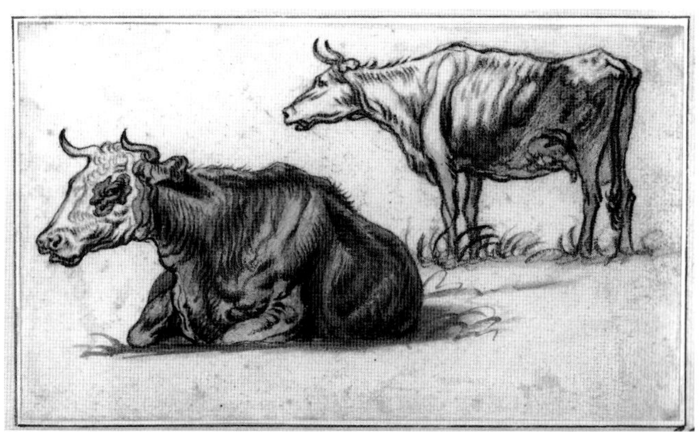

31

Reinier à Persijn after Jacob Gerritsz Cuyp,

Cows with a sleeping herdsman by a farmhouse, 1641.

Engraving, 130 x 193 mm.

32

Aelbert Cuyp, *A cow lying and a cow standing.*

Black chalk, grey wash, 90 x 148 mm.

Rijksmuseum, Amsterdam

In the final analysis, Cuyp was not a master of animal portraiture like Paulus Potter, whose works include the famous painting of *The bull* in the Mauritshuis in The Hague. Cuyp's drawings and etchings are essentially studies, attempts to define an animal's coat or to record the native cattle in swift lines. In his paintings, the cattle play a leading role on more than one occasion, but there is usually also something else going on. In his *Cows in a river* (fig. 30) the main focus is on the little group of animals, on their reflections in the water and on the fall of the light on their bodies. But there is also a towering sky with edgily painted clouds and a peaceful panorama with a little church and a single small boat on the flat calm water. As a painter of animals, Cuyp is at his best here, but a painting like this could not possibly be described as a portrait of cows.

The question arises as to how such work by Cuyp should be interpreted. It has been argued that the cattle in the landscape should be seen as a gift from God. The animals were created to serve man and indeed the Dutchman of the 17th century, with grassy meadows and healthy cattle, regarded himself as truly blessed. It is an interpretation that may perhaps hold water for a riverbank scene with a dairymaid milking a cow, but it does not seem to hold the key to five cows by the water's edge or to a traveller asking a herdsman the way. It has also been suggested that in his paintings Cuyp wanted to depict the Dutch Arcadia, a country where life is good and the herdsmen and shepherdesses have all the time in the world to go courting. This interpretation seems equally far-fetched for a landscape with cows, but it might stand up for a work like the *River landscape with horseman and peasants* (fig. 54). One reason why neither possibility is really appropriate might be that each wants to provide a solution for all the problems. They are, however, related, and the common element is perhaps the most important: insight into the qualities of one's own environment, in which the question of whether this is God-given country or country that is as delightful as distant Italy or the Arcadia of Ancient Greece is really not very relevant.

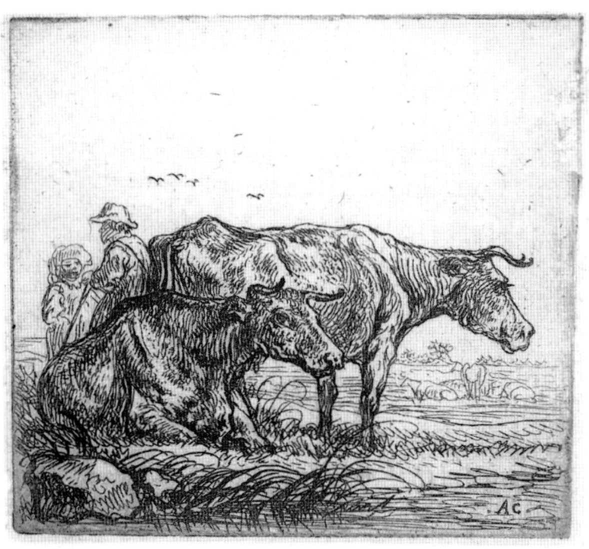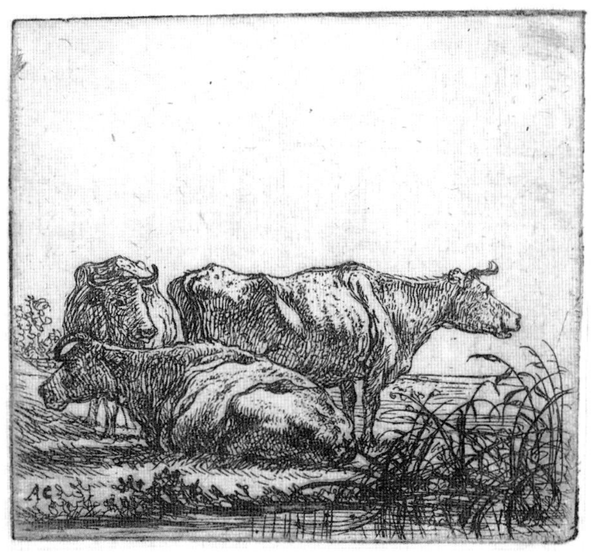

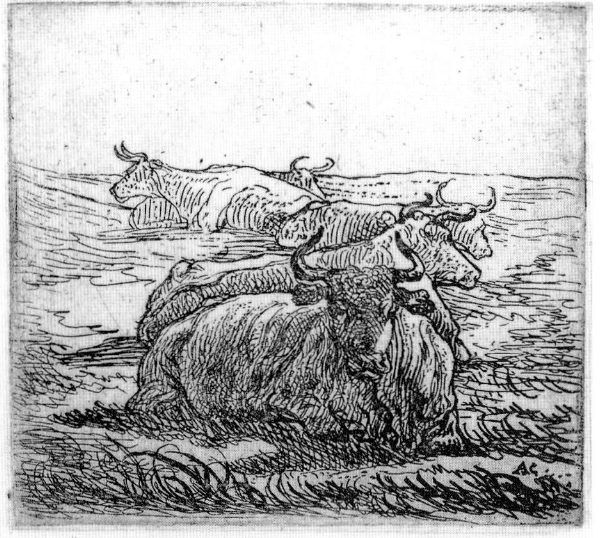

33

Aelbert Cuyp, *A cow lying and a cow standing,*
with two herdsmen. Etching, 67 x 74 mm.
Rijksmuseum, Amsterdam

34

Aelbert Cuyp, *Three cows.*
Etching, 67 x 74 mm.
Rijksmuseum, Amsterdam

35

Aelbert Cuyp, *Five cows lying down.*
Etching, 67 x 74 mm.
Rijksmuseum, Amsterdam

There can be no doubt that Cuyp enjoyed depicting his home city, Dordrecht, from an early age nor that he found buyers for his pictures of the city with its characteristic church tower. Around 1647 Cuyp must again have embarked on a trip on the Oude Maas to make drawings of the city. One of the panoramic cityscapes he made on this occasion is *Dordrecht viewed from the north, with the Grote Kerk and the Groothoofdspoort* (fig. 36). In this work he looked at Dordrecht from the middle of the water, where the Oude Maas, the Merwede and the Noord meet. The main motif on the left is the Groothoofdspoort, while further to the right and more distant, the Grote Kerk dominates the city. Further right again, we can make out the entrance to the Nieuwe Haven with its swing bridge. The view of the Oude Maas is largely blocked by a sailing boat crossing in front of it while the buildings on the Zwijndrecht side can be seen on the right. Cuyp originally set the drawing down sketchily, probably concentrating on the skyline. During this session he drew two other sections of the skyline in the lower left corner, a stretch of the city wall with houses – apparently the section to the right of the gate that has disappeared behind the sails – and a few more houses, which he evidently tried to erase and then attempted to conceal with a reflection in the water. He almost certainly added the other reflections at the same time. The cloudy sky was undoubtedly added by a later owner in the 18th century, probably at the same time as the elegant inscription.

Cuyp used the drawing for two famous painted views of Dordrecht (figs. 37 and 38). In both of them the skyline is partly concealed behind a sizable sailing vessel. In one painting (fig. 37) the composition of the ships and the quay is virtually identical to the drawing, although the fall of the light differs slightly. In the other (fig. 38), he made a more obvious use of the central section with the windmill. For both paintings, Cuyp also drew inspiration from a drawing of a freighter and a timber raft (fig. 39).

The role of Cuyp's drawings as preparatory studies for his paintings is clearly illustrated by these two sheets. The panoramic drawings of cityscapes are often regarded as completed products in their own right, work that has been perfected to such an extent that it is hard to doubt their autonomous nature. The fact that in the bottom left-hand corner of this sketch Cuyp drew in rows of houses that he considered necessary for the picture of the city makes it clear that he attached great importance to topographical completeness. What's more, he made repeated use of the skyline in the drawing. He went back to this sheet, for example, for *The Maas at Dordrecht* (fig. 42). This points to its being studio stock.

Cuyp's drawing *A freight boat and a timber raft on calm water* (fig. 39) is definitely a real preliminary study. In it Cuyp was looking for the right placement of the boats and the timber raft, and was not yet certain whether he would show the big freighter with or without a sail. It may have been while working on this drawing that he struck on the motif of the transhipment of barrels – something which would certainly not have been done with the vessel in full sail and which would in any event have happened near a quay and not in the middle of the water as it is in the two paintings. Elements of this working drawing found their way into several paintings. The sloop sailing away appears in another painting (fig. 41), where it is depicted with the same fall of the light.

Aelbert Cuyp's use of this drawing in these two paintings (figs. 37, 38) also provides food for thought as to the relationship between these two impressive works. In principle, this drawing most nearly resembles the painting in Ascott House. There on the right, after all, slowly sailing away, is the sloop, which is absent from the painting in Kenwood. Moreover the two workmen on the left on the raft – there are probably two and they are probably on the rearmost raft – are similar in pose. In both paintings Cuyp added a helmsman next to the rudder at the stern of the raft. Nevertheless it seems more likely that Cuyp initially conceived the painting in Kenwood, a monumental work in a traditional format, and that he subsequently extended the

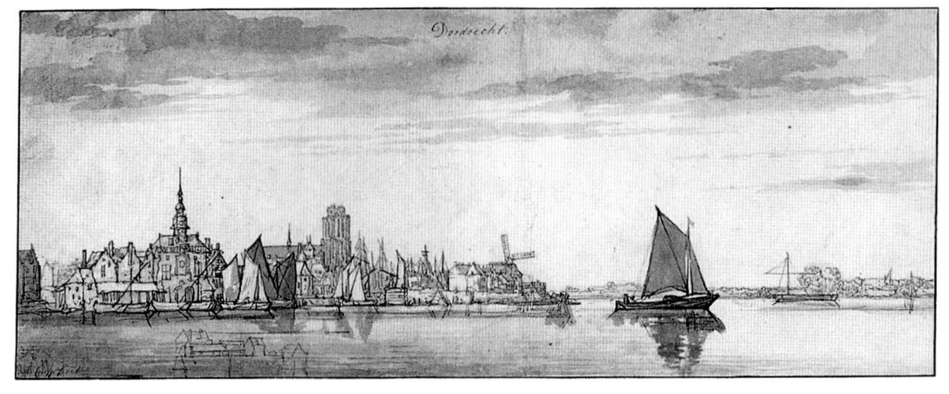

36

Aelbert Cuyp,

Dordrecht viewed from the north, with the Grote Kerk and the Groothoofdspoort. Black chalk, grey wash, 187 x 460 mm. Rijksmuseum, Amsterdam

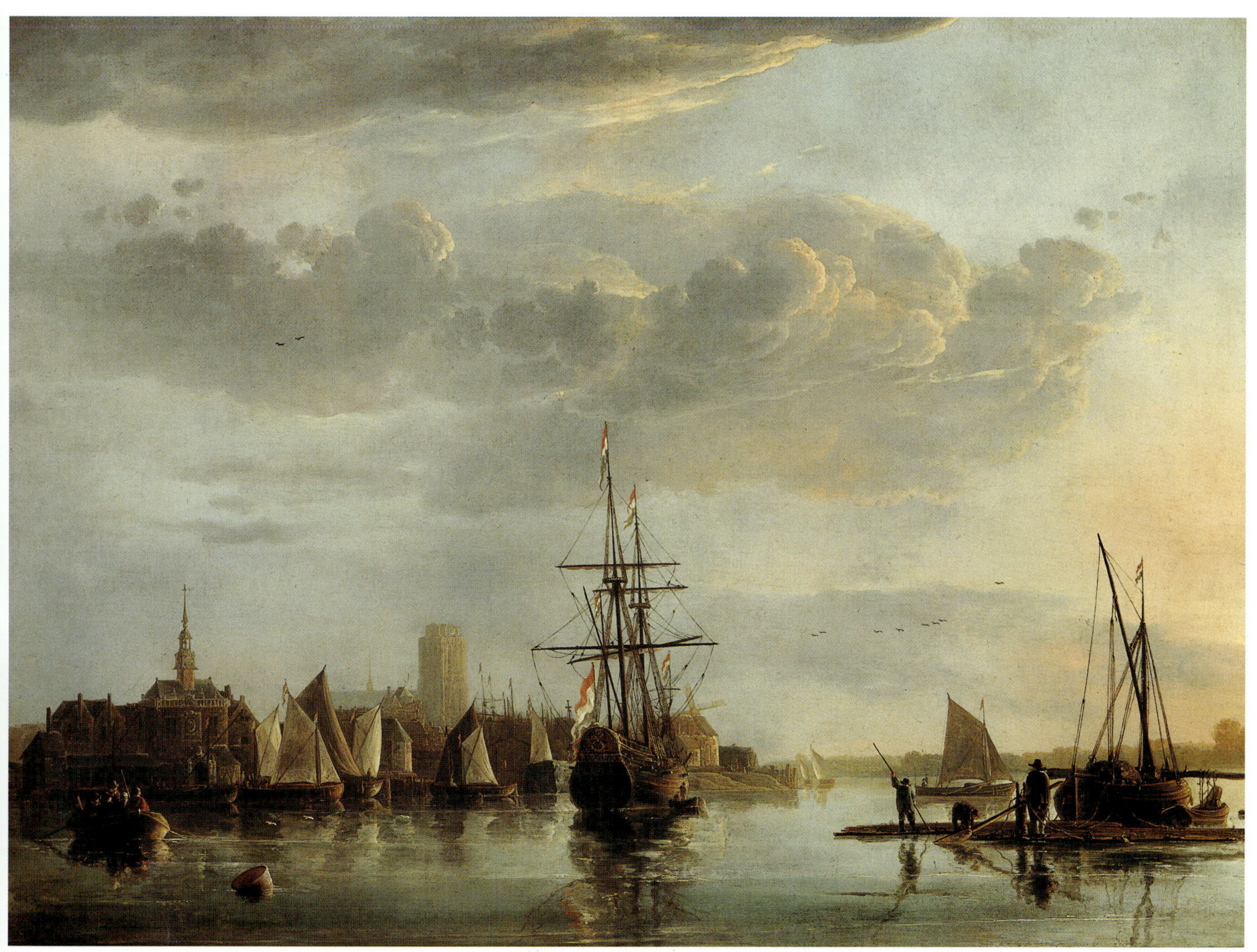

37

Aelbert Cuyp, *Dordrecht viewed from the north*.

Canvas, 97.8 x 137.8 cm.

English Heritage (The Iveagh Bequest, Kenwood)

composition in the width in his painting in Ascott House. One indication of this is the sailing boat that blocks the view on the right in the drawing. In the painting in Kenwood this vessel is in the same place, half behind the timber raft. In the painting in Ascott House (fig. 38) he originally showed the boat in the same way – this earlier form has become visible over the years – but then gave it a more westerly course to make it follow the other boats. This is part of his attempt to broaden the composition. The vegetation on the left, which extends widthways but yet creates depth, was added with the same aim in mind. The plants at the water's edge offered him more opportunities than the rowing boat he added in the left foreground of the other painting. Most daring, however, is his addition of two figures in the little sailing boat on the right. They look at the sunset, thus suggesting an even wider panorama.

As we have noted, Cuyp also used the drawing for his painting of *The Maas at Dordrecht* (fig. 42). It is thought that this depicts the massing of the fleet that took place off Dordrecht in 1646 at the request of Prince Frederick Henry. The size of the fleet becomes even more overwhelming when one also looks at the pendant of this painting, *Dordrecht viewed from the north* (fig. 40). Prominent citizens of Dordrecht undoubtedly played an important role in organizing this naval review and it is undoubtedly in this circle that we must seek the patron who, with these monumental canvases, owned a truly impressive suite of works.

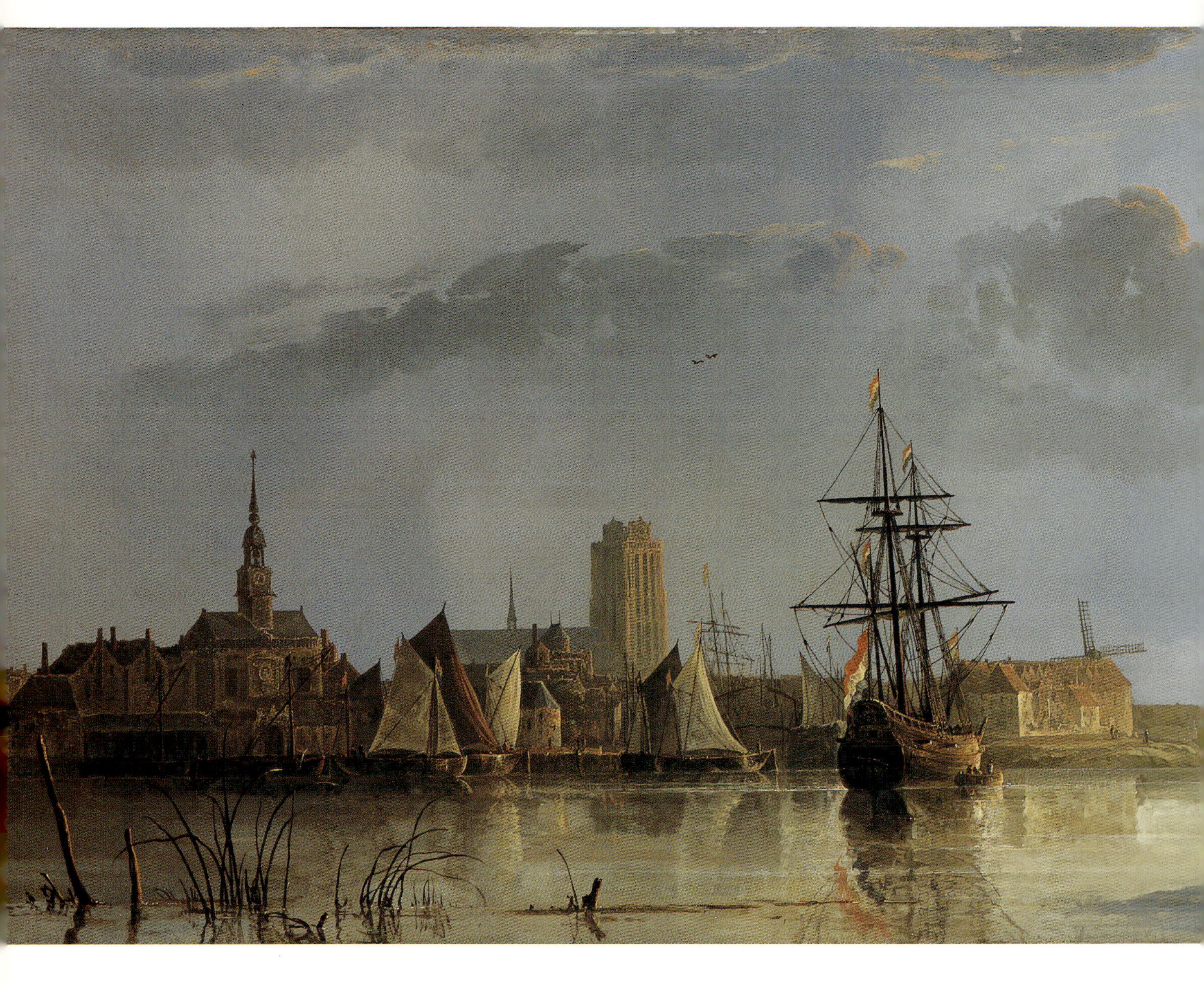

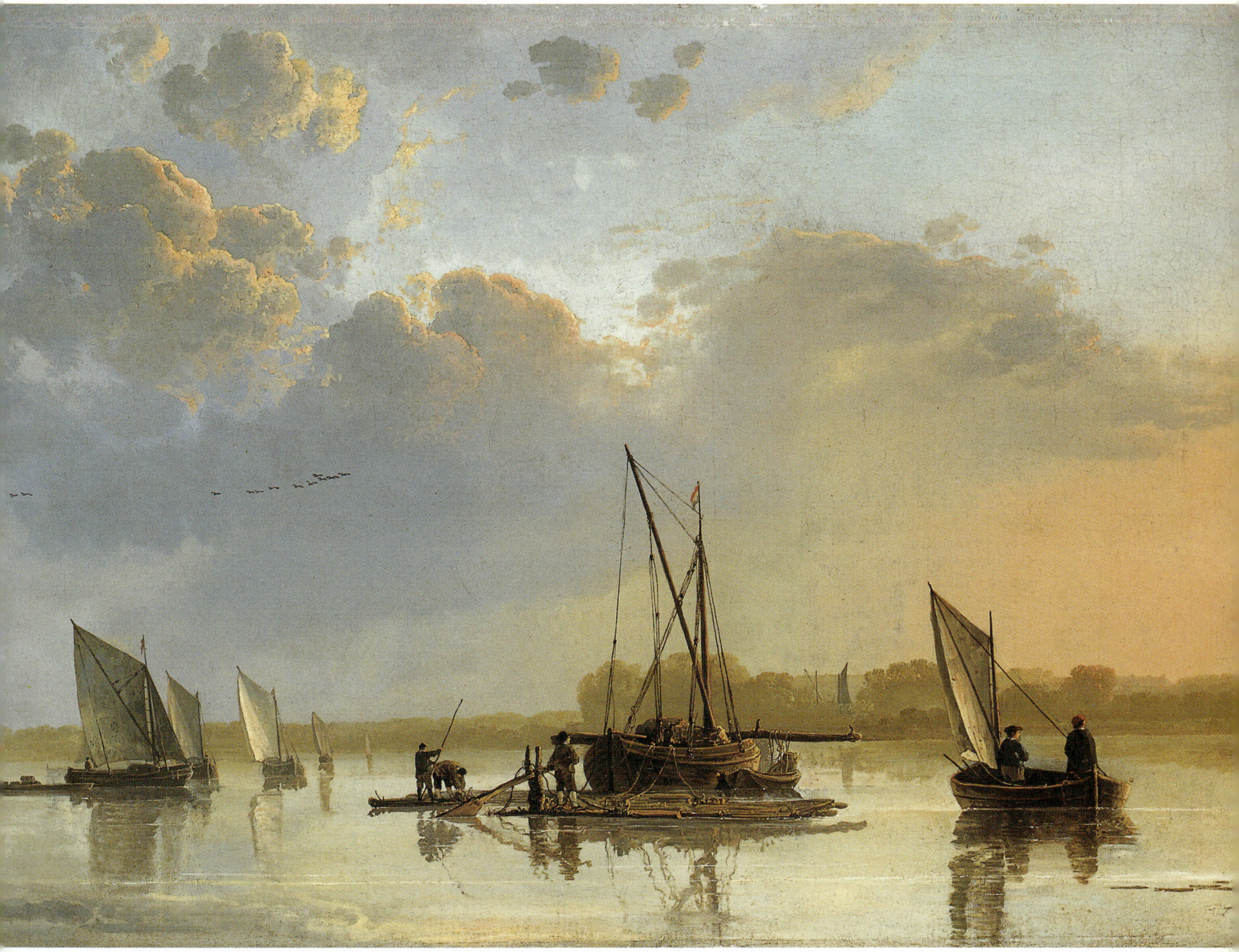

38

Aelbert Cuyp, *Dordrecht viewed from the north.*

Canvas, 68.5 x 190 cm. The Rothschild Collection

(The National Trust), Ascott

39

Aelbert Cuyp,

A freight boat and a timber raft on calm water.

Black chalk, grey wash, 168 x 254 mm.

The British Museum, London

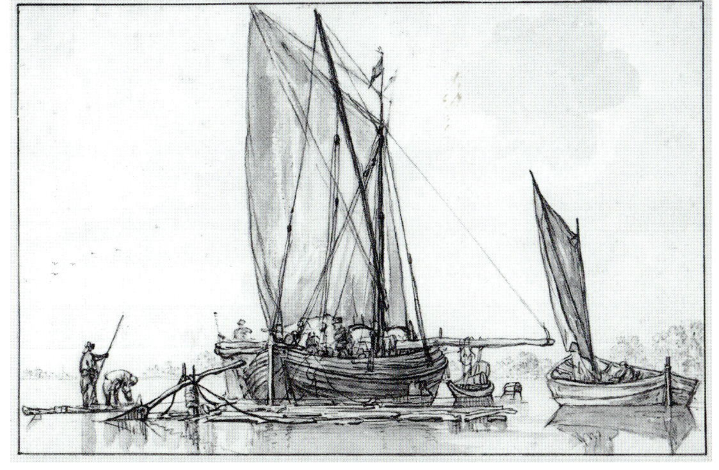

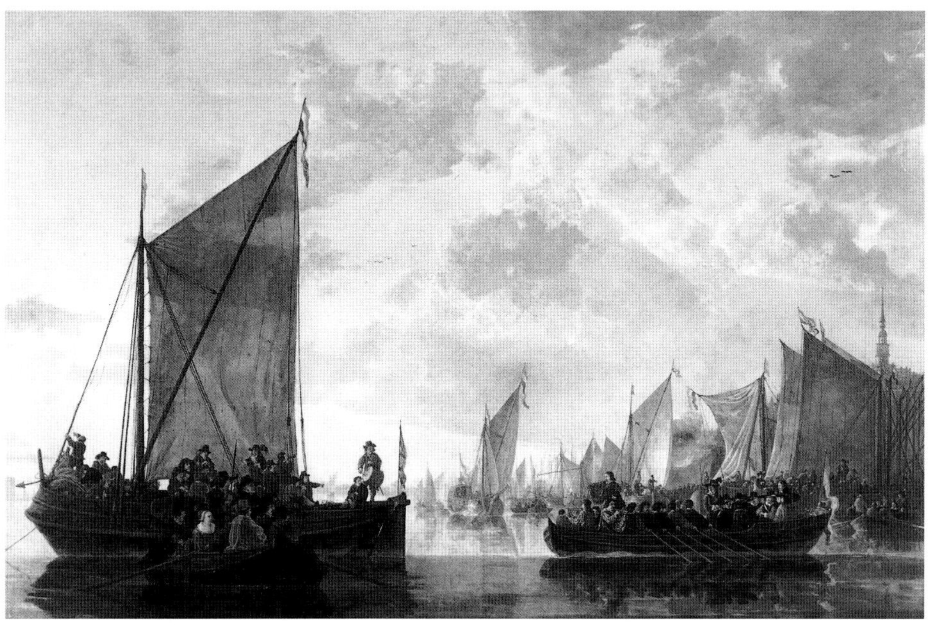

Aelbert Cuyp, like his father, served a
Dordrecht clientele. Cuyp's customers
were ambitious and well-to-do Dordrecht
citizens who were on the point of being
admitted to the upper echelons of the city
government. The paintings, in which they
play leading roles, as it were confirm their
social pretensions. A good example is the
equestrian portrait of Pieter de Roovere
(fig. 43). He was lord of the manor of
Hardinxveld, where the salmon fishery in
which he had legal rights was an important
source of income. He is shown on horseback, dressed in a distinguished-looking
but imaginary outfit, and is being present-
ed with a salmon by a fisherman wearing
waders. In the background we can see an
impressive house on the bank of a river,
probably the Merwede. On this side of the
water a gentleman of standing (undoubtedly De Roovere again) supervises the haul-
ing in of fishing nets, while a groom with
a saddled horse comes running up from
the right. There can be no mistaking
De Roovere's claims to rank.

As his father had achieved success with
a combination of portrait and landscape,
so Aelbert sought his own form for group
portraits, in which the sun-drenched fanciful landscapes so characteristic of him
played a prominent role. Most of the works
in which Aelbert used this combination
were equestrian portraits, like *Michiel and
Cornelis Pompe van Meerdervoort with their tutor*
(fig. 44), a charming yet at the same time
curious work. The painting is listed in
an inventory of the Meerdervoort house,
near Zwijndrecht, across the river from
Dordrecht, as hanging 'on the chimney-
breast', 'in the nursery'. In a later inventory
the painting is described more extensively
as a chimneypiece work, 'portraying
masters Michiel and Cornelis Pompe van
Meerdervoort going hunting with their
tutor, groom, etc'. The painting must have
been made around 1653, the year in which
the elder brother, Michiel, died. It is there-

40	41 ▼
Aelbert Cuyp, *Dordrecht viewed from the north*.	Aelbert Cuyp, *Moored boats*.
Canvas, 114 x 166 cm.	Panel, 70.5 x 89 cm.
The Rothschild Collection	The Rothschild Collection
(The National Trust), Waddesdon	(The National Trust), Waddesdon

30

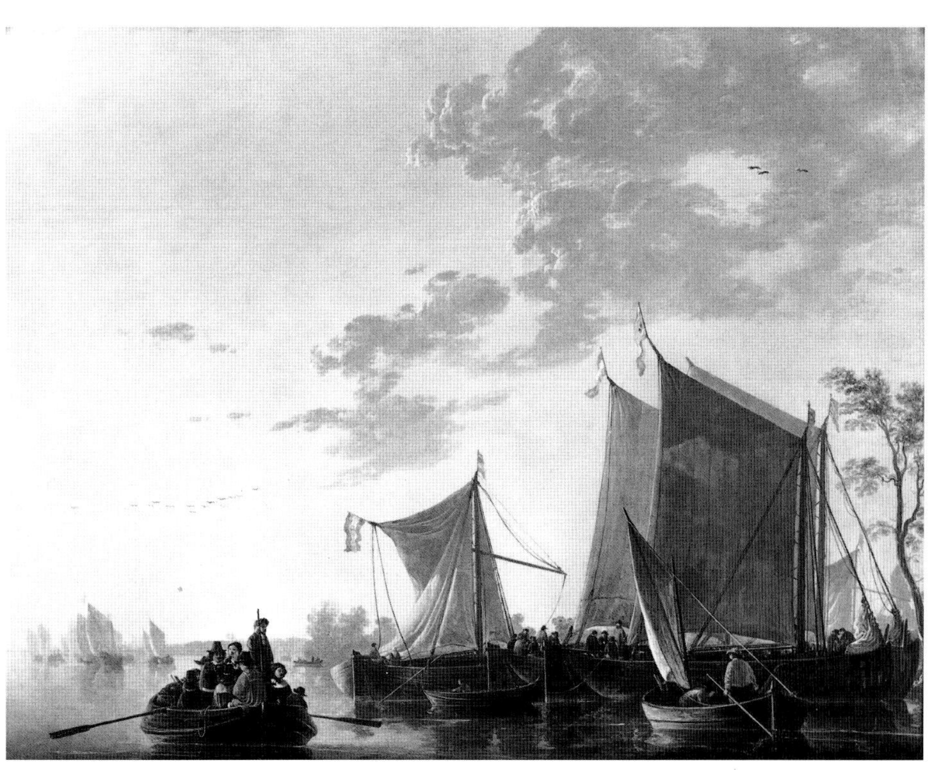

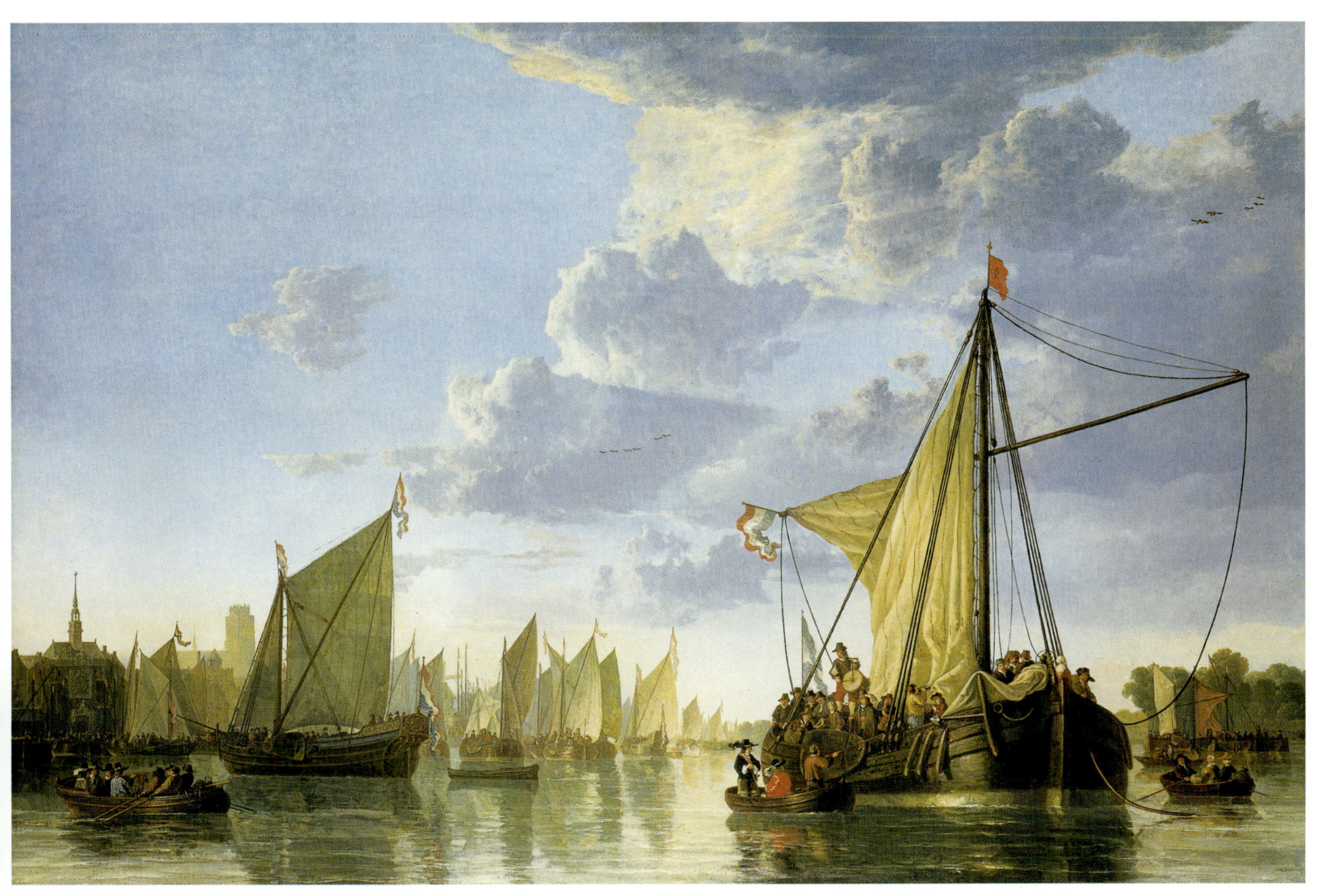

42

Aelbert Cuyp, *The Maas at Dordrecht*.

Canvas, 115 x 170.2 cm.

National Gallery of Art, Washington

(Andrew W. Mellon Collection)

fore quite possible that the painting is in fact a memorial portrait, made for the younger son to keep the memory of his dead brother alive. The two boys are accompanied by their 'riding instructor' and a groom, and are shown in fanciful costumes in front of a probably non-existent castle. In the background there is an accurately depicted landscape of the Rhine near the Elterberg, which Cuyp based on a drawing (fig. 46) that he made shortly after 1650 during a trip to Nijmegen and Cleves. The attractive light (although contradictory because the shadows indicate light coming from the left, whereas the background suggests the rays of the sun coming from the right rear), the bright palette, the sometimes odd proportions (as in the boy in the middle), the fine horses and the clumsily painted dogs all point to a complicated commission that the painter was not able to pull off satisfactorily in all respects. A possible explanation for some of the compositional awkwardness could be related to the young rider in the centre, who appears to be a later addition. It is possible that the recent accident which cost the young man his life compelled Cuyp to revise the plan for this painting and to place Michiel in the centre of the work.

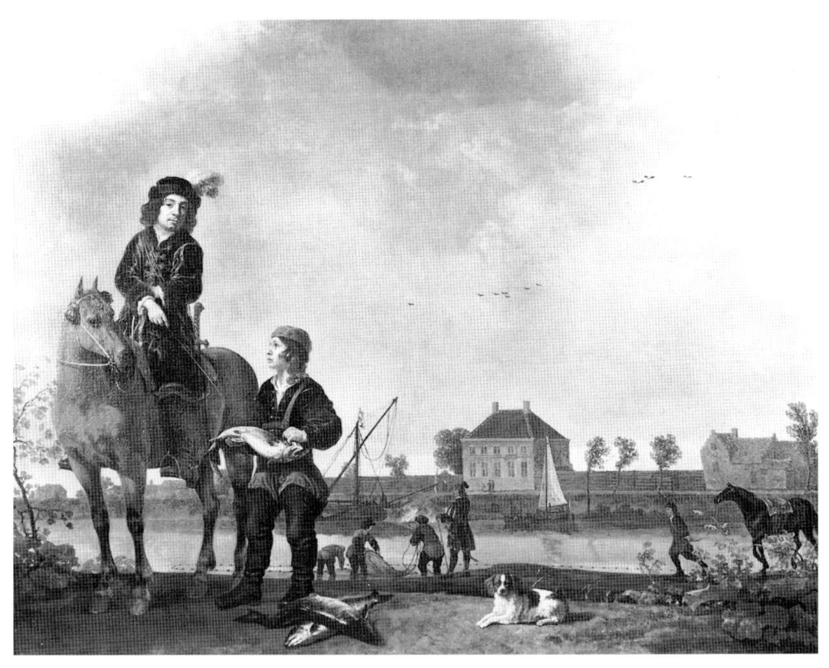

43

Aelbert Cuyp, *Pieter de Roovere as Lord of the
Manor of Hardinxveld*. Canvas, 123.5 x 154 cm.
Mauritshuis, The Hague

44

Aelbert Cuyp, *Michiel and Cornelis Pompe van Meerdervoort
with their tutor*. Canvas, 109.8 x 156.2 cm.
The Metropolitan Museum of Art, New York
(The Friedsam Collection)

32

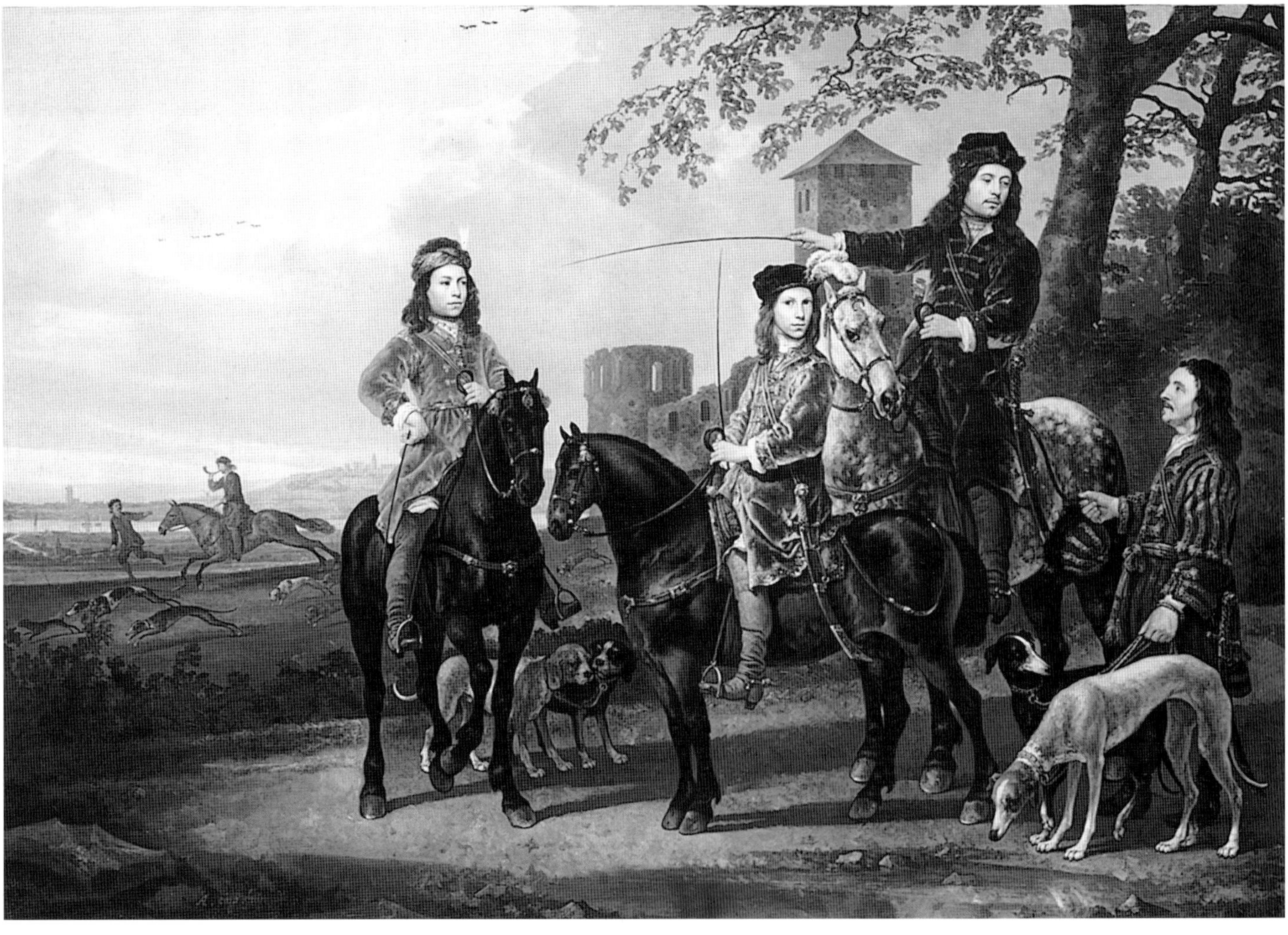

Cuyp's success as a painter of horses is nicely demonstrated by a likewise simultaneously fine and clumsy painting in Rotterdam, *Groom with horse and half-hidden horseman* (fig. 45). The patron, undoubtedly the rider pulling his boots on behind the horse, had his horse, groom and dog immortalized in this painting. The unusual and witty solution Cuyp chose here has meant that this painting has not always been recognized as an equine portrait, as we see from a title like *Man seated behind a horse*, which ignores the wonderful quality of the rendition of the horse.

Paintings like these must have been commissioned. This is not, however, to say that Cuyp worked only to order. He must also have made numerous landscapes for the open market. All the same, the great flood of exports of Cuyp's paintings to other countries in the 18th century originated chiefly in Dordrecht, which means that Cuyp's works were primarily bought by people in his home city.

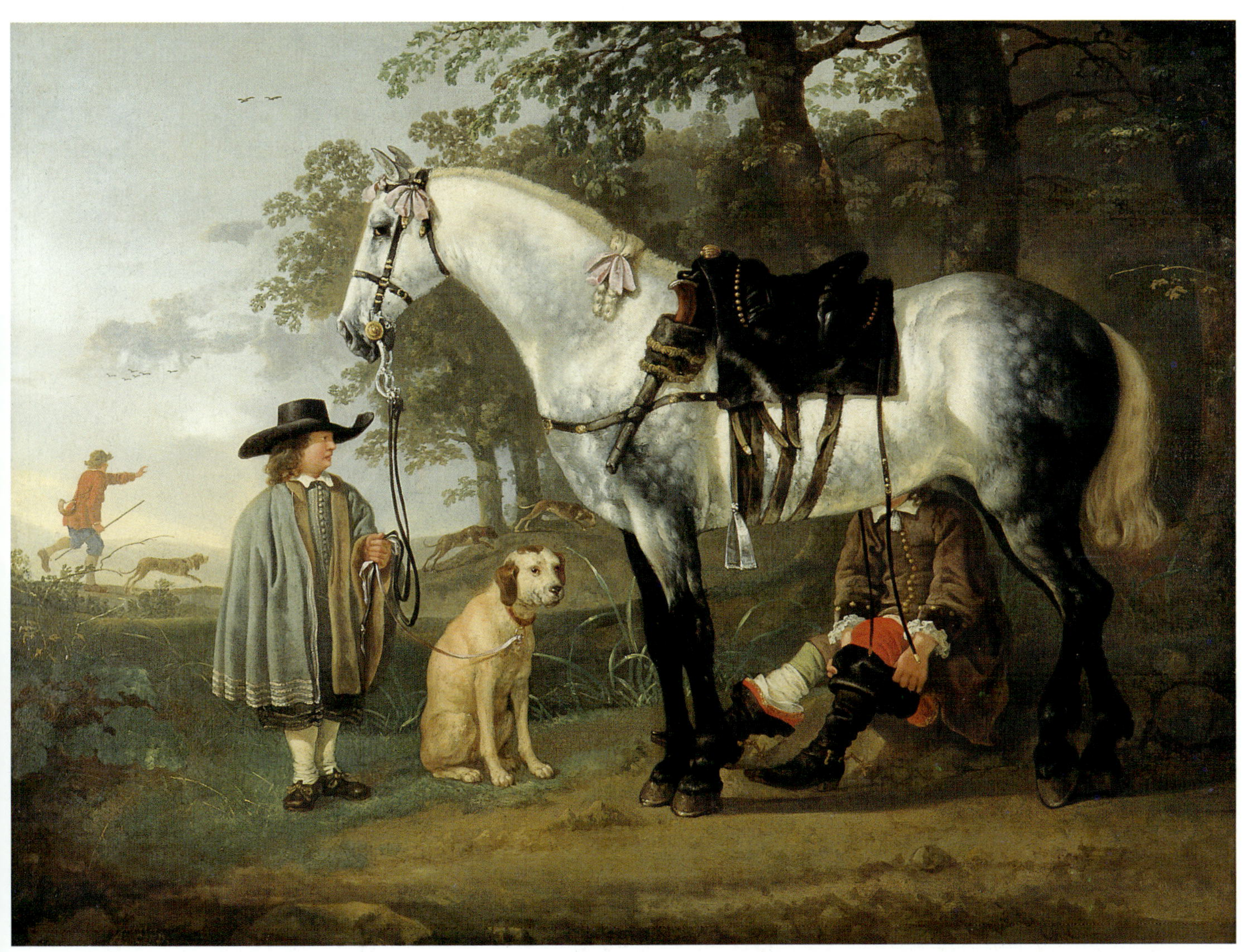

45

Aelbert Cuyp, *Groom with horse and half-hidden horseman*.

Canvas, 91 x 117 cm.

Willem van der Vorm Fundatie,

Museum Boijmans Van Beuningen, Rotterdam

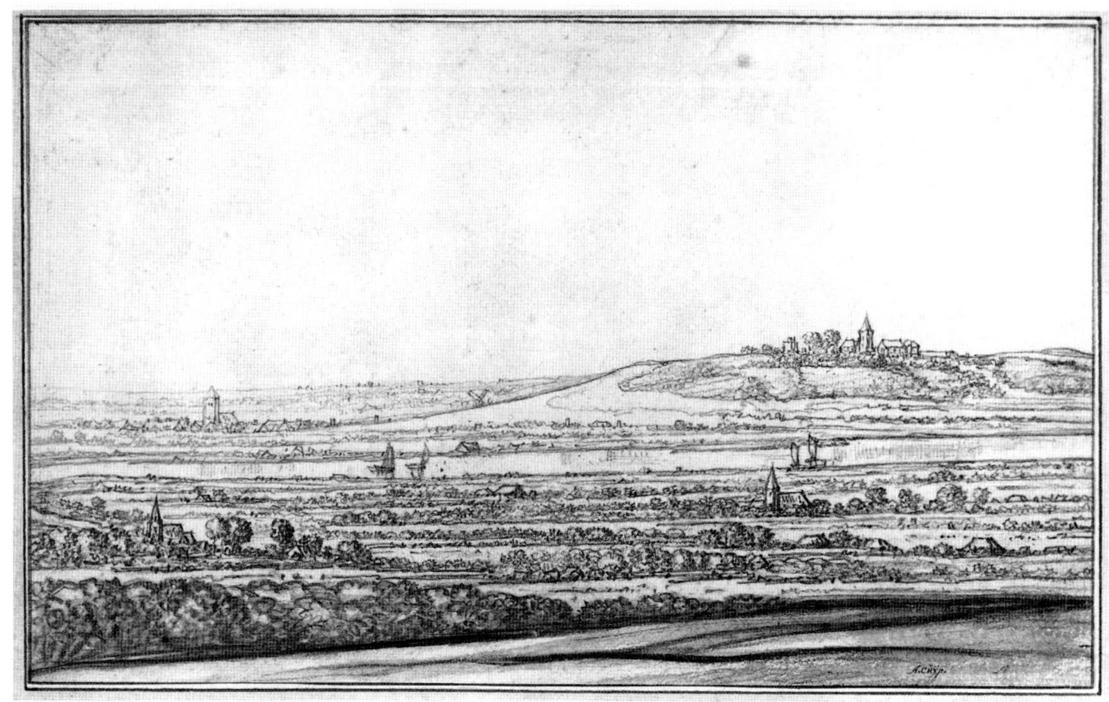

46
Aelbert Cuyp, *The Rhine Valley with the Elterberg*. Black chalk, grey wash, graphite, 149 x 240 mm. Collection Frits Lugt, Institut Néerlandais, Paris

34

47
Aelbert Cuyp, *Part of a view of Cleves*, verso of fig. 50. The British Museum, London

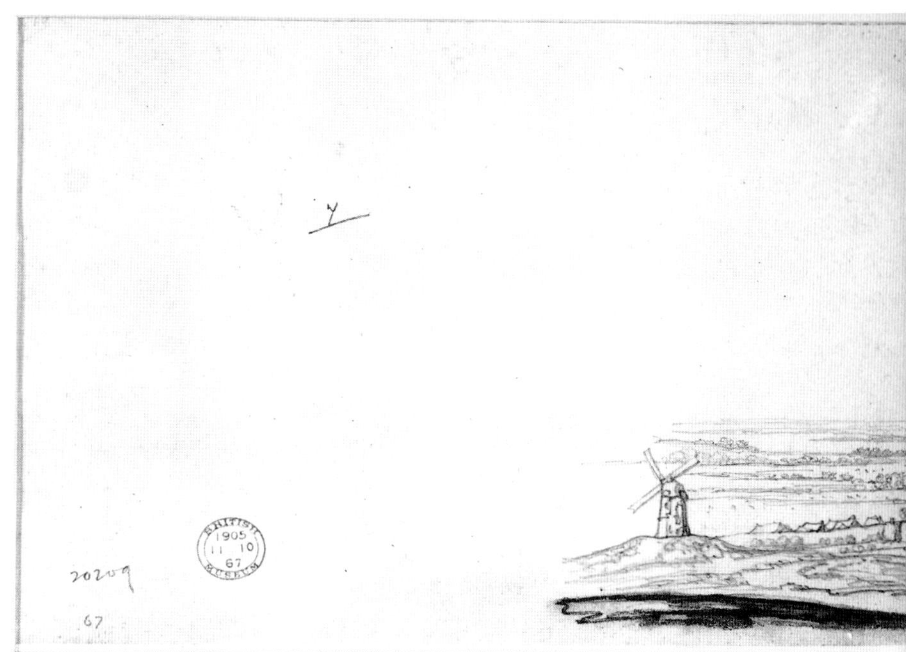

FURTHER TRAVELS

Following his early visits to Utrecht, Rhenen and the area around Kalkar, soon after 1650 Cuyp again travelled eastward, this time to Nijmegen, Cleves and the surrounding countryside. This journey resulted in a series of drawings made in a sketchbook that probably measured 20 by 28 cm. The subjects in the sketchbook are predominantly towns and cities, like Nijmegen and Cleves, imposing ruins, like Ubbergen Castle, and landscapes with views over the Rhine valley with tall hills in the distance, like the Elterberg or the Monterberg. The drawing of Cleves (fig. 49) in this series provides us with some very valuable information. Framing lines have been drawn on it, probably indicating where the sheet was to be trimmed – something that has indeed been done with most

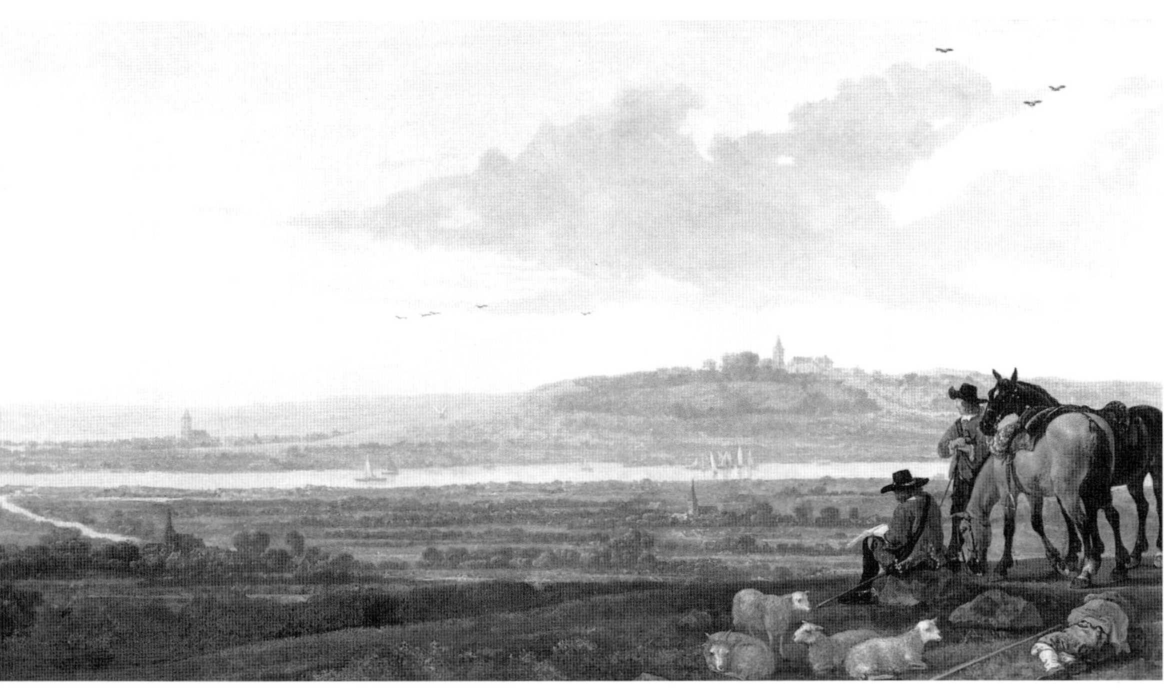

Aelbert Cuyp,
The Rhine near the
Elterberg with an artist.
Panel, 47.5 x 80 cm.
Woburn Abbey, Woburn,
Bedfordshire

49
Aelbert Cuyp, *Cleves viewed from the Galgenberg.*
Black chalk, grey wash, graphite,
190 x 278 mm. Rijksmuseum, Amsterdam

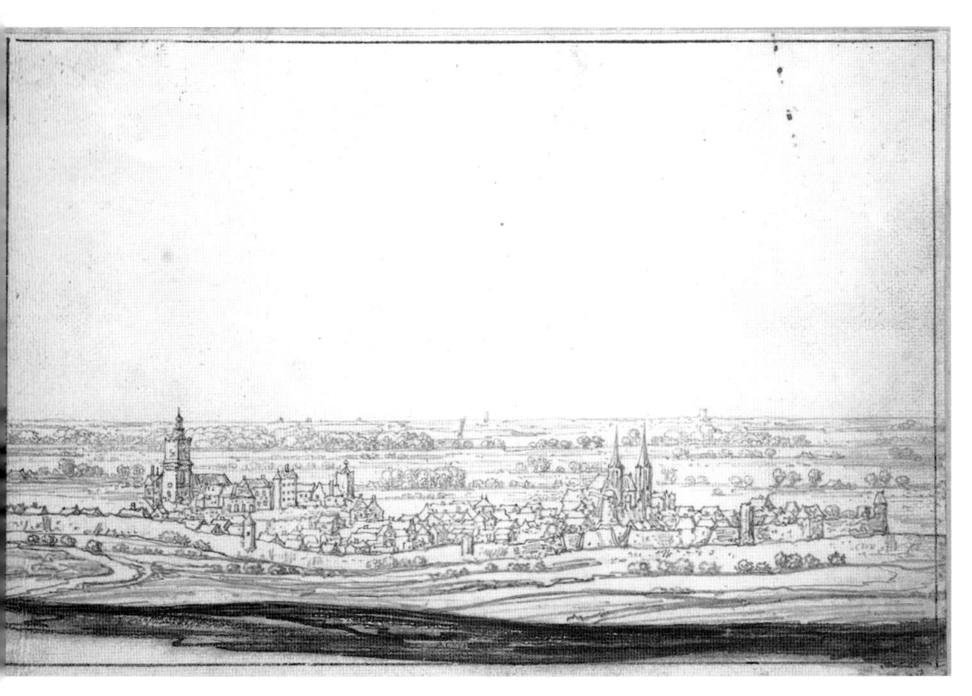

of the drawings. It is one of the largest sheets in the series and it is quite likely that the original size of the sketchbook has been retained in this case. *Cleves viewed from the Galgenberg* also provides us with a useful point of reference for dating the series: one of the towers on the city wall, the Raventurm, collapsed in 1652 and was then demolished. Cuyp consequently must have made the drawings before this date – probably only shortly before.

We know that *Cleves viewed from the Galgenberg* comes from a sketchbook because of a supplementary sketch on the back of another sheet (fig. 47). Cuyp evidently wanted to record another small area near Cleves, which he apparently thought necessary for positioning the city in the landscape. The idea must only have occurred to him later, so he continued on the back of the previous page. From the Galgenberg, where he recorded the view of Cleves, Cuyp also drew the view to the southeast, looking towards Kalkar and the Monterberg. He must have made drawings on the Sternberg to the west of Cleves before his trip up the Galgenberg, because *The Rhine Valley with Schenkenschans Fort* (fig. 50), made at that spot, has the sketch of the surroundings of Cleves on the back (fig. 47). Shortly before this he had drawn the exceptionally fine *Rhine Valley with the Elterberg* (fig. 46), likewise from the Sternberg. A comparison of these drawings reveals that Aelbert Cuyp had an extraordinarily sure hand as a draughtsman; he was consistent in style, too, as we can see from the manner in which the clumps of trees in the valley are rendered. When he chose, he could alternate his subtle drawing style with a much more powerful one, as the broadly executed foregrounds show.

Cuyp reprised the hymn in praise of magnificent views that seems to be sung in these drawings in a few paintings which, because of the presence of an artist, seem to have a personal character. His painting *The Rhine near the Elterberg with an artist* (fig. 48) is based on the view of the valley and the Elterberg (fig. 46), now in low sunlight, with two dismounted horsemen, one of whom sits with a sketchbook on his lap, drinking in the view. Although the reality content of Cuyp's painting should not be taken too literally – artists are much more likely to have climbed these hills on foot rather than on horseback – the delight in the view is palpable. The convincing pseudo-realism of this painting stands in sharp contrast to the almost absurd imaginary setting of which this same landscape formed a part in *Michiel and Cornelis Pompe van Meerdervoort with their tutor* (fig. 44).

Cuyp used the drawings in the sketchbook for a number of exceptionally fine paintings, like his magnificent work *The Valkhof, Nijmegen, viewed from the northwest* (fig. 51). Nijmegen, like Dordrecht, was an important subject for Cuyp. Since he also used the city as the backdrop to a monumental marine work, similar to the paintings of ships off Dordrecht (figs. 40, 42), we can perhaps assume that this is why Cuyp travelled east again. The journey from Dordrecht to Nijmegen – by boat in any event – is not a particularly complicated one. There must also have been contacts between the Dordrecht timber merchants – Dordrecht was an important staple market for timber – and Nijmegen, where the timber rafts from Germany were steered up the Waal towards Dordrecht. In the painting (fig. 51), which is rather smaller than most of Cuyp's views of Nijmegen, he combines the magnificent Valkhof, built for Charlemagne, with the warehouses on the quay, the Belvedere and a windmill that stands out in silhouette on the brow of the next hill. Herdsmen and fishermen in the foreground lend the scene a rural atmosphere, while the strong red accent of the jacket worn by one of the herdsmen sparks the otherwise subtle palette. The colourful sky and the sun's rays pouring in from the east set the distant view of the river aglow and imbue the landscape with a prosperous and peaceful air.

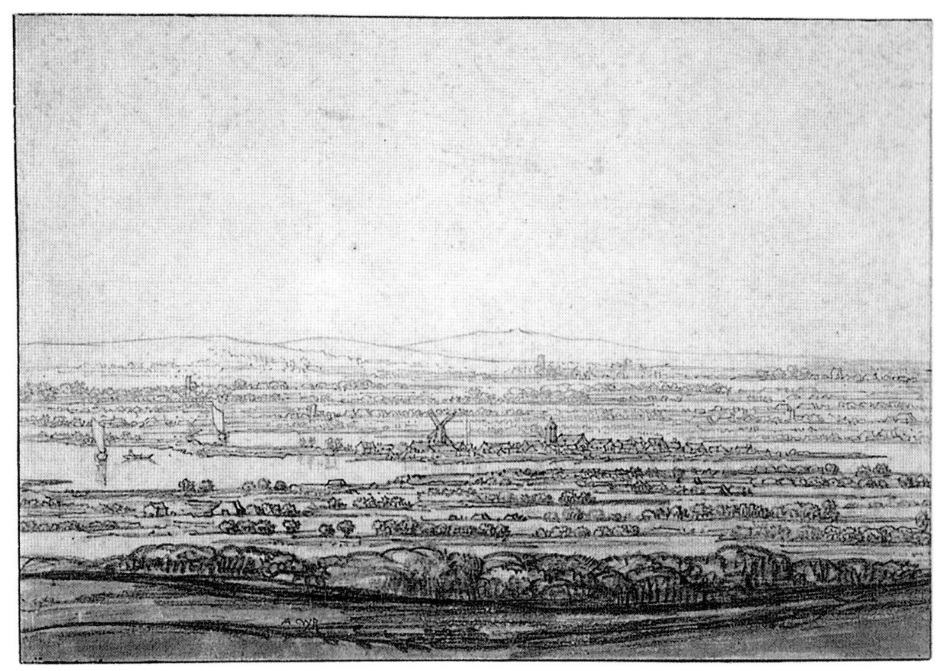

50

Aelbert Cuyp,

The Rhine Valley with Schenkenschans Fort. Black chalk,

grey wash, graphite, 174 x 245 mm.

The British Museum, London

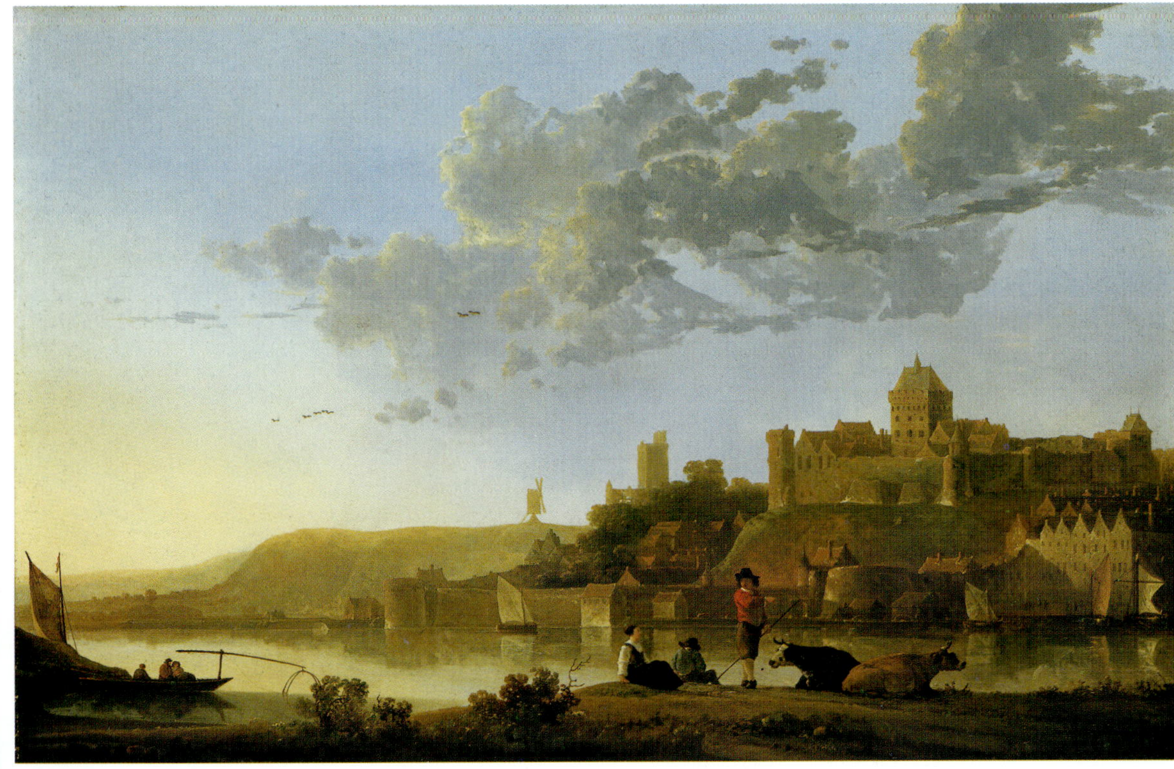

Aelbert Cuyp,

The Valkhof, Nijmegen,

viewed from the northwest.

Panel, 49 x 73.7 cm.

Indianapolis Museum

of Art, Indianapolis

THE MAJOR LATE WORK

It was the same steep hills beyond Nijmegen (fig. 51) that inspired Cuyp's great *River landscape with two horsemen* (fig. 52). The Rhine, which once flowed at the foot of these hills and caused the severe erosion in the landscape, now lies much further to the north. A few old streams and the Wylermeer are all that now remain of what must once have been an important waterway. By Cuyp's day the streams were already quite insignificant. The tall hills on the right are the Wylerberg and further on, past the tower of the church in the village of Wyler, is the massif on which Cleves stands. The citadel in the distance is an embellished version of the ruins of Kranenburg Castle. Even the inn, which survived into the 19th century as the Startjeshof Inn, is accurately depicted. Compared with the topographical manipulation that he so evidently indulged in in *Cattle and herders, with the*

Mariakerk, Utrecht (fig. 8), Cuyp followed the landscape impression he had recorded in the preliminary study (fig. 53) reasonably carefully. Nevertheless the *River landscape with two horsemen* is anything but a topographically accurate depiction of a specific place. Cuyp was concerned to capture the contrast between the hills and the low-lying land, the mood of a warm summer evening, the suggestion of a few moments of rest on a long journey. He cleverly used the small lake to suggest a wide, meandering river on the left. The sky, with the fanning tatters of cloud so characteristic of Cuyp, accentuates the heat of the summer evening.

As in the large painting in the Rijksmuseum (fig. 52), in the *River landscape with horseman and peasants* (fig. 54) the intimate world of herdsmen with cows and horsemen pausing on their journeys is combined with a compelling view. Whereas the fore-

ground of the Amsterdam painting is sometimes thought to be rather empty, in this work it is full of anecdotes. A horseman, probably an officer of the state army, stands by a herdsman who points the way with a broad gesture. A walker with a stick over his shoulder continues down the road that the rider hesitates to take and meets a shepherdess with a small boy, guardians of a flock of sheep. The rather strange meeting of people has a parallel in the meeting between the animals: the cow that evinces an interest in the horse and the flock and herd that are about to pass each other. What is the story in this painting? Is the horseman being turned back or is the herdsman actually pointing out to him the distant town that he will be able to reach by following the water's edge? Or is the rider's attention being drawn to the hunter in the left foreground, who is on the point of firing at a little group of wild ducks?

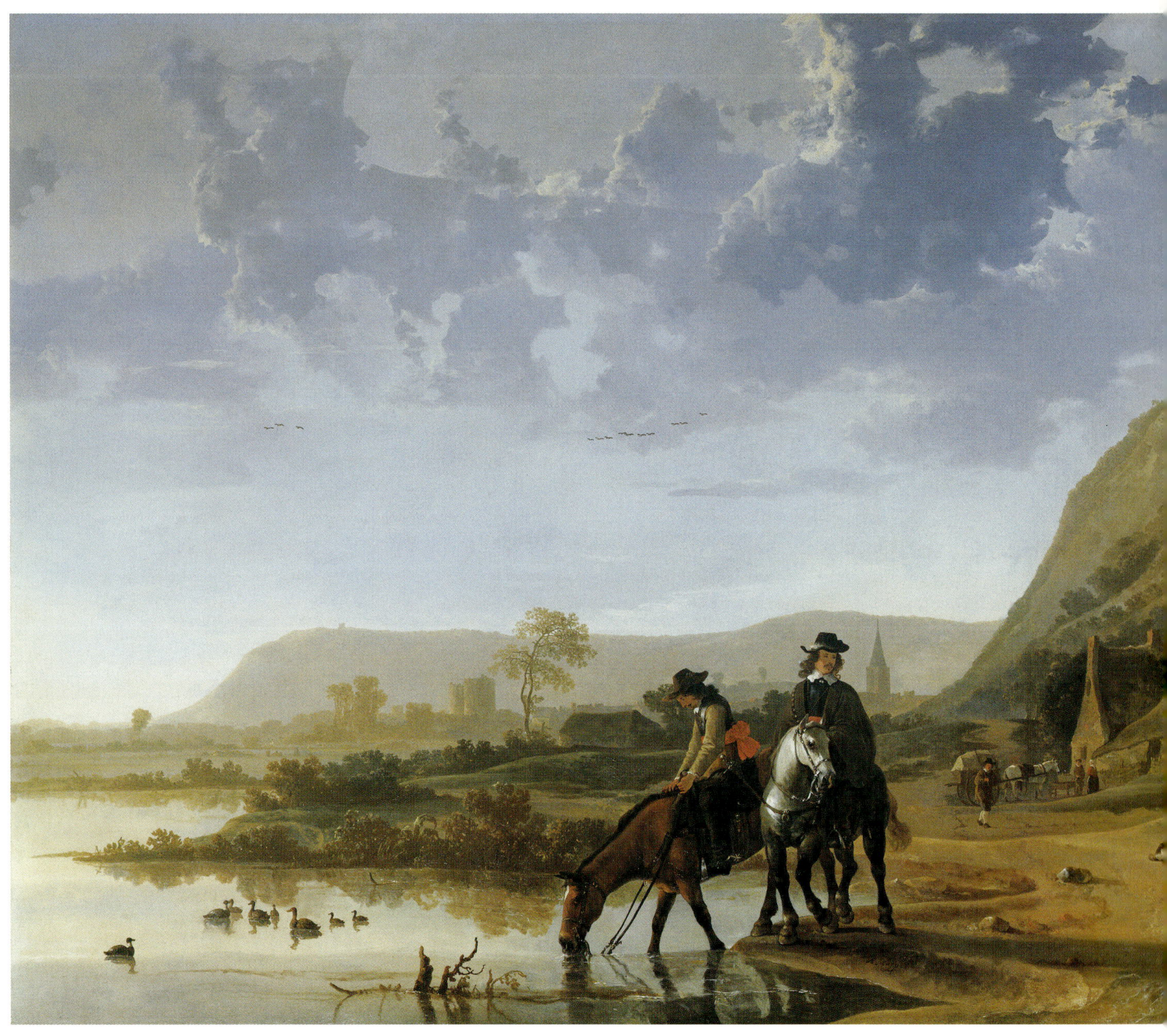

Discovering him in the painting, the viewer momentarily experiences the shock that will reverberate through the scene when the shot rings out.

The landscape, too, takes unexpected turns. The clump of tall trees to the left of the road and the trunk of the tree on the right, which enclose the composition, inexorably lead the viewer's eye to the right, where the road into the distance is suggested, running alongside the river to the town and the mountains. While the high hills in the previous painting make a fairly improbable impression, here the mountains appear to be entirely imaginary. Here, moreover, Cuyp attracts the viewer's attention with the lushness of the foreground vegetation: beautifully executed branches and foliage with both dark and brightly lit passages.

For his depictions of the horse and the cows, Cuyp fell back on a number of studies that he had probably made some time earlier and also used for several other paintings. He took the cow with the white head lying down from a simple little sketch (fig. 55). Cuyp must have found the serene peace of cattle in a landscape – an essential element of his more mature paintings – in drawings like this. On another sheet

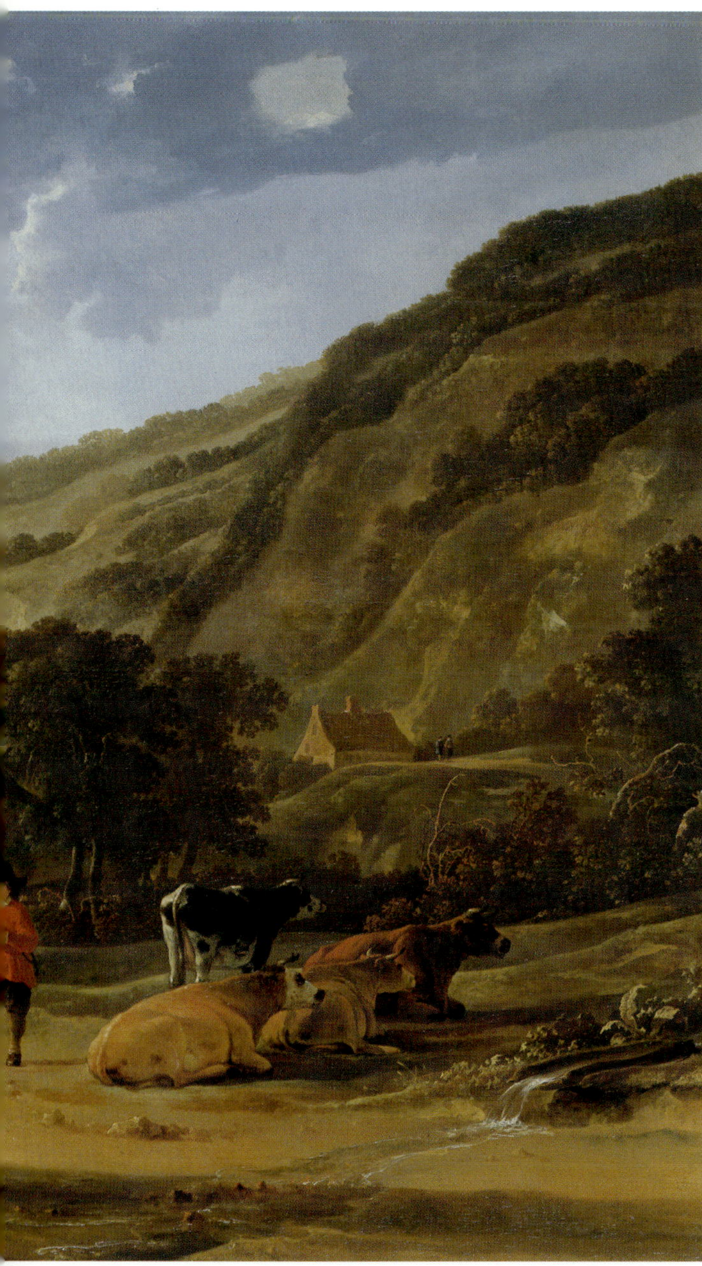

52

Aelbert Cuyp,

River landscape with

two horsemen.

Canvas, 128 x 227.5 cm.

Rijksmuseum,

Amsterdam

53

Aelbert Cuyp, *The hills near*

the Wylermeer between

Nijmegen and Cleves.

Black chalk,

162 x 245 mm.

Formerly Duits art

dealers, London

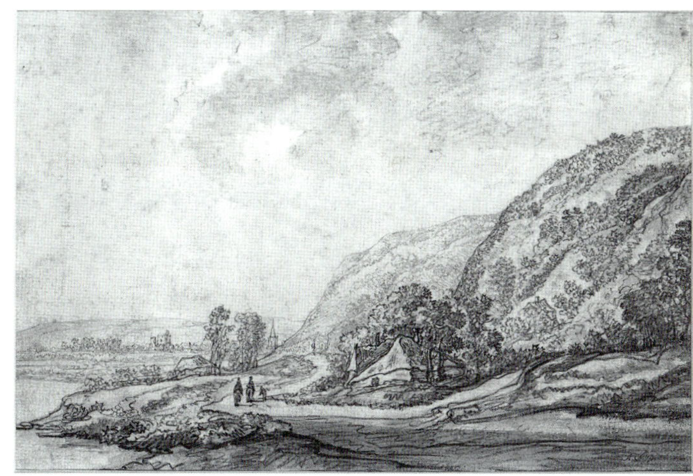

(fig. 56) he made a study of the brown and white cow which is partly concealed behind the black and white beast. Cuyp even kept the pattern of markings on the head in the painting.

The horse in this drawing largely corresponds with the grey horse in the painting. There are minor alterations in the position of the legs and the pose of the head, but the most important change is that Cuyp has transformed the animal from a weary carthorse into a proud steed.

Although there are few clues as to the dates of these two monumental paintings – we can say little more than that they were painted after 1650, possibly around 1655 – the two works are generally seen as the grand finale of Cuyp's oeuvre.

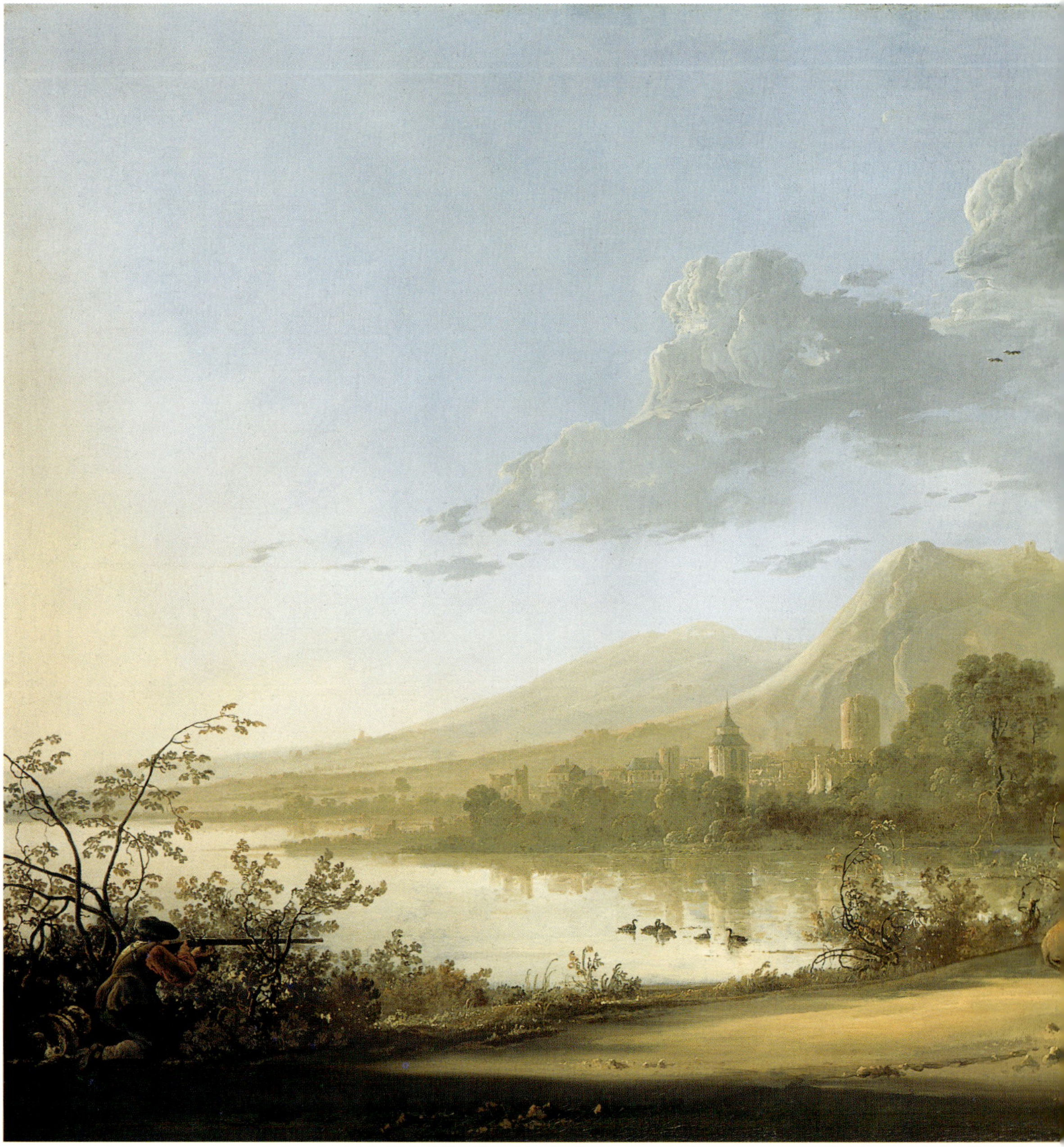

54

Aelbert Cuyp, *River landscape with horseman and peasants.*

Canvas, 123 x 241 cm.

The National Gallery, London

55

Aelbert Cuyp, *A cow lying down.*

Black chalk, grey wash, 76 x 133 mm.

Private collection, Amsterdam

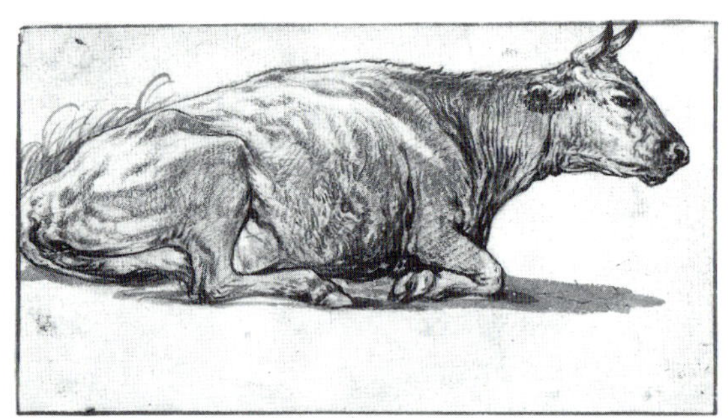

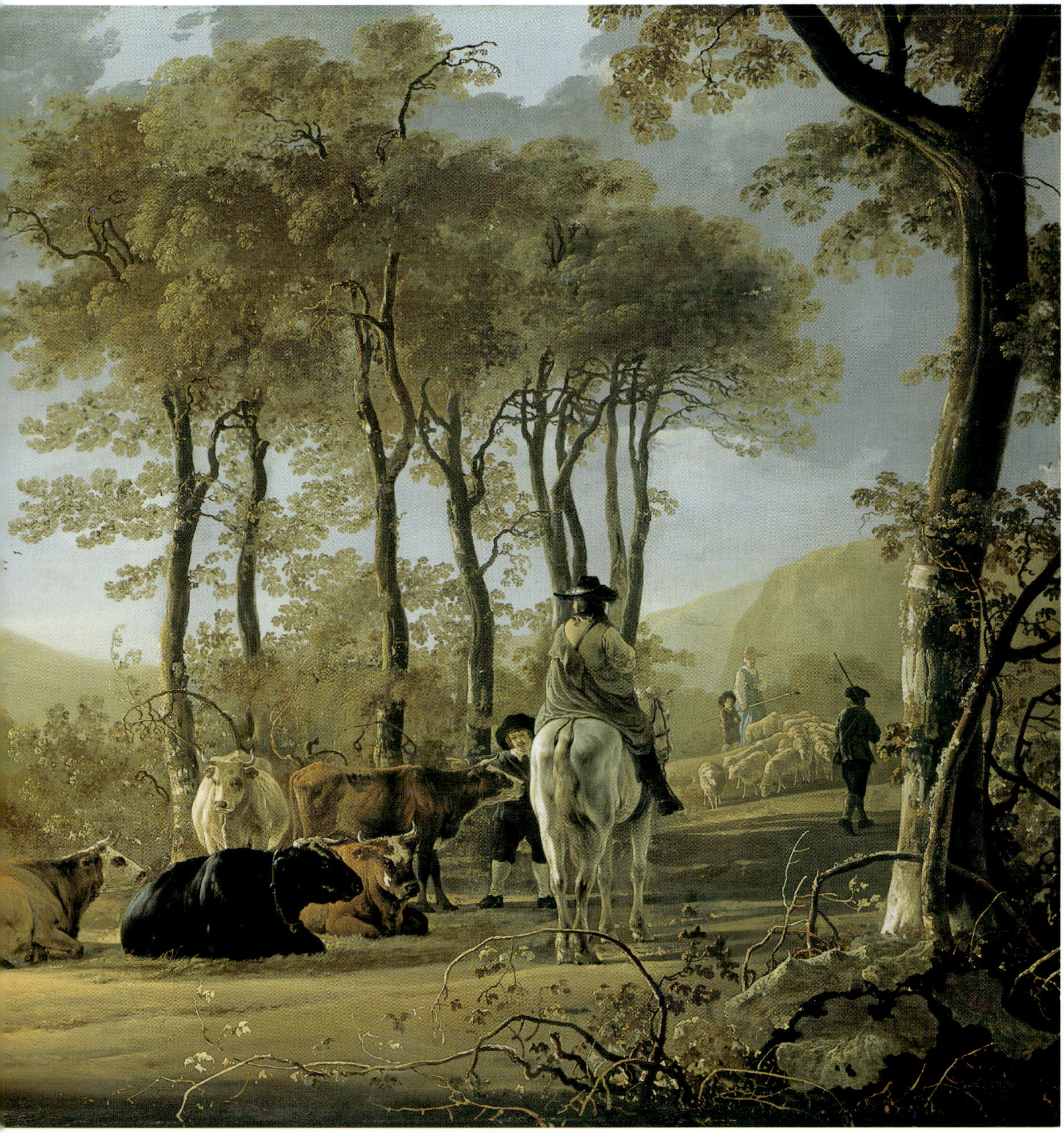

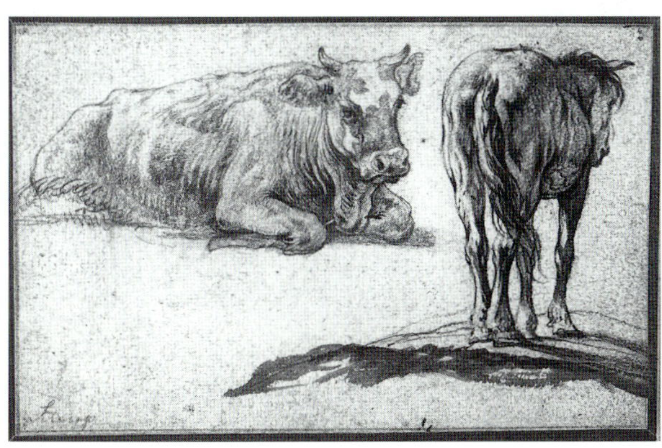

56

Aelbert Cuyp,

Studies of a cow and a horse. Black chalk,

grey wash, graphite, 84 x 125 mm.

Collection Frits Lugt, Institut Néerlandais, Paris

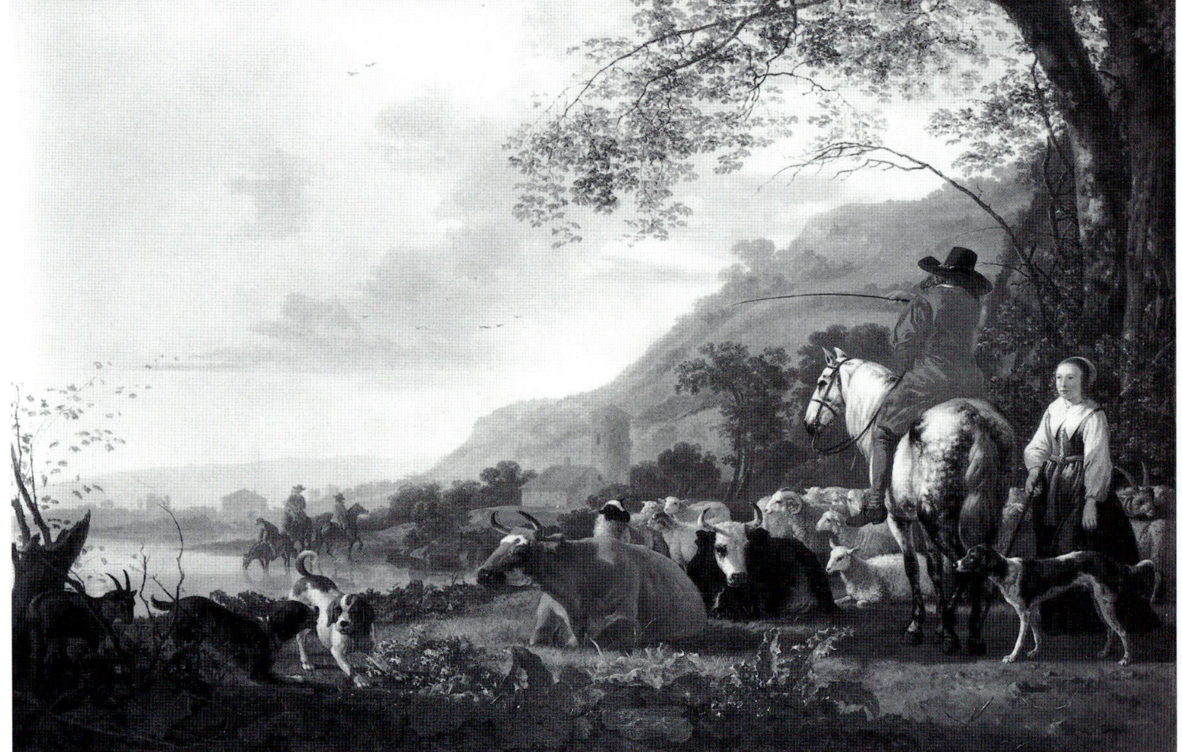

57

Attributed to

Abraham van Calraet,

A hilly river landscape

with a horseman talking

to a shepherdess.

Canvas, 135 x 201 cm.

The National Gallery,

London

42

ASSISTANTS AND FOLLOWERS

Aelbert Cuyp's work was very highly
sought-after, both in his lifetime and after-
wards. His popularity has meant that Cuyp
was widely imitated and this in turn has
led to significant problems of authenticity.
Estimates of works supposedly painted by
Cuyp range from around 175 to 1600, and
attribution was certainly not made any
easier by the master himself, who probably
also signed work by pupils.

The question as to whether Aelbert
Cuyp ran a studio has barely been considered in art historical literature. There are
no documents relating to a 'workshop'
or to pupils. Only Abraham van Calraet,
Cuyp's 'look-alike' and undoubtedly
Cuyp's pupil, has occasionally prompted
debate. There are good grounds for assum-
ing the existence of studio assistants: Jacob

58

Studio of Aelbert Cuyp,

Evening landscape with

herdsmen and cattle.

Canvas, 105 x 103 cm.

Rijksmuseum,

Amsterdam

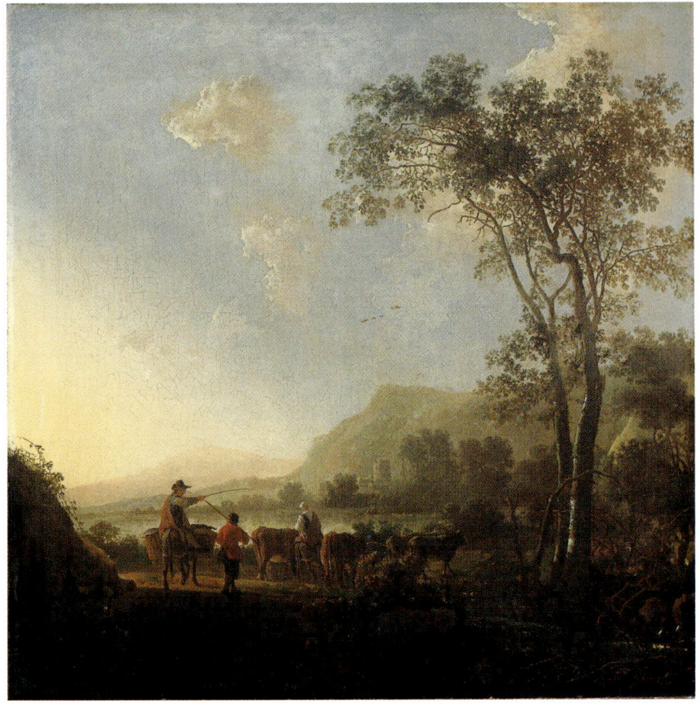

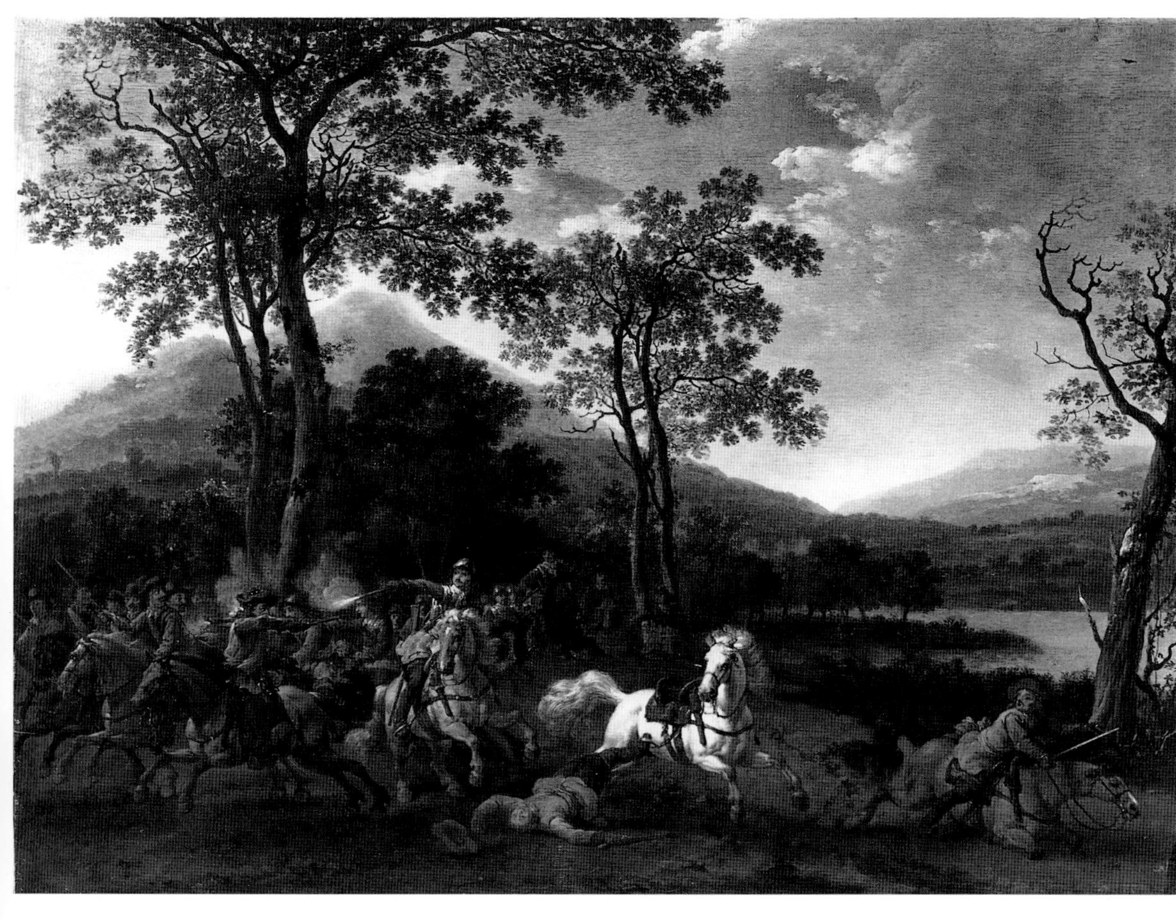

43

Cuyp used pupils and assistants, and it seems obvious that his son would have done the same.

Among the paintings in the Rijksmuseum in the style of Cuyp – three of which certainly date from the 17th century – there is the painting that for generations was the prime example of Cuyp's work, the *Evening landscape with herdsmen and cattle* (fig. 58). The painting is signed and apparently has the most impeccable provenance one could imagine: it hung over the door in the house of Pieter Onderwater, the man who married Cuyp's only daughter. And yet the painting really does not fit into Cuyp's oeuvre. The subject is Cuyp (herdsmen with cattle in a river landscape surrounded by high hills in the evening light, the herdsman pointing the way with his crook), the mood is Cuyp (the drowsy feel of a late summer's evening

with those typically fanning clouds), the detailing is Cuyp (branches and foliage in the foreground, as it were a threshold to the central plane where the action takes place, a red jacket to attract the attention and a white cap catching the light) and yet it is not a Cuyp (there is too little contrast between the clouds and the evening sky, and the branches and foliage are not vigorous enough). There can in fact be only one solution: it was made in the studio by an assistant, under the master's supervision.

We see just how confusing the situation is in the large *Hilly river landscape with a horseman talking to a shepherdess* in the National Gallery in London (fig. 57), often praised and described in such terms as 'one of the best and most important works of Cuyp's maturity'. Two of the most important experts on Cuyp's work, however, have

attributed it to Abraham van Calraet (1642-1722). The work does, it is true, have great qualities, it is close to Cuyp, but it handles the motifs in too decorative a manner. The horsemen in the water in the background are borrowed from the Amsterdam painting (fig. 52); the red jacket worn by the rider on the right is no longer a potent colour accent but a red that has the same value as the blue of the shepherdess's dress. The cow in the middle is like the cattle in Cuyp's work, but lacks the robustness of form. The most telling argument, however, is that Van Calraet used the same horse in several paintings that he signed. If we assume that the paintings in Amsterdam and London (figs. 52, 54) are important mature works by Cuyp and that the work discussed here was painted by Van Calraet, then we have to consider the possibility

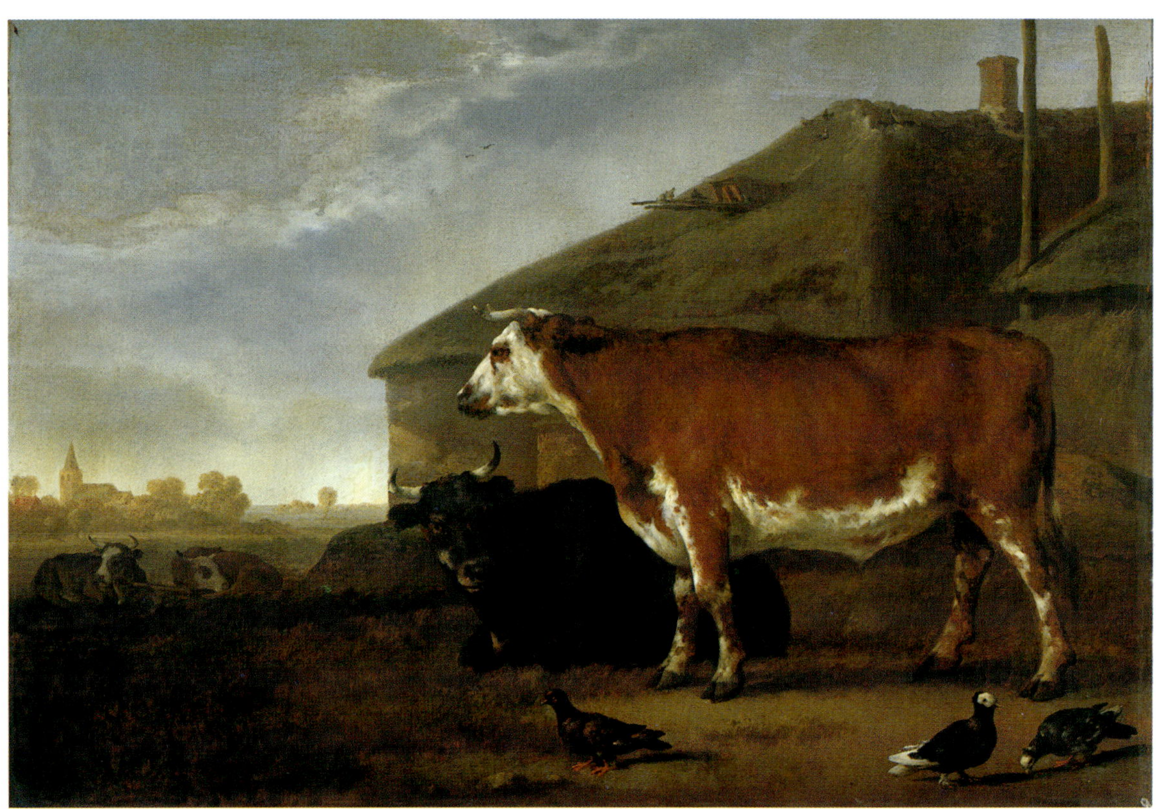

that around 1660 Van Calraet executed important commissions in Cuyp's name, possibly as the senior assistant in the studio.

Abraham van Calraet himself compounded the confusion. He signed his work 'A.C.', a signature that Cuyp also used occasionally, for example in his etchings (figs. 33-35). It is therefore not surprising that characteristic works by Van Calraet, signed with his initials, have been attributed to Cuyp in the past. For example, when he portrayed a bull with some cows and three doves by a farmhouse (fig. 60), he captured the foreground animals well, but he was unable to achieve the harmonious peace of Cuyp's cattle.

The *Cavalry skirmish* signed 'A.C.' (fig. 59) is also Abraham van Calraet's work. In it, more than in the other two works, he has found a form of his own. He was able to define his figures rather more easily than Cuyp, with small, highly contrasting

60 ∧
Abraham van Calraet, *Cattle.*
Panel, 39.5 x 55.5 cm. Rijksmuseum, Amsterdam

61
Jacob van Strij,
Landscape with cattle drover and shepherd.
Panel, 57 x 83.5 cm. Rijksmuseum, Amsterdam

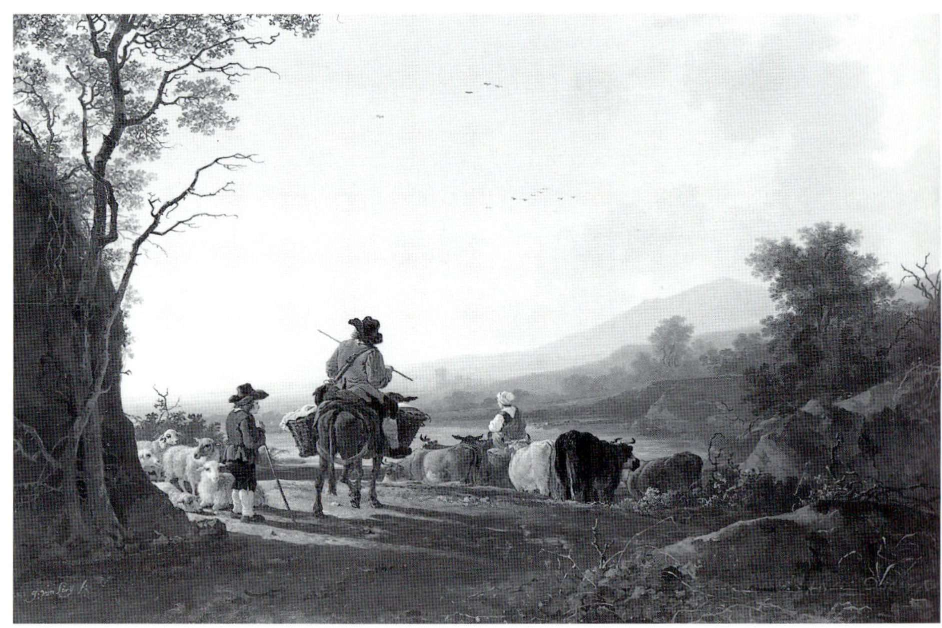

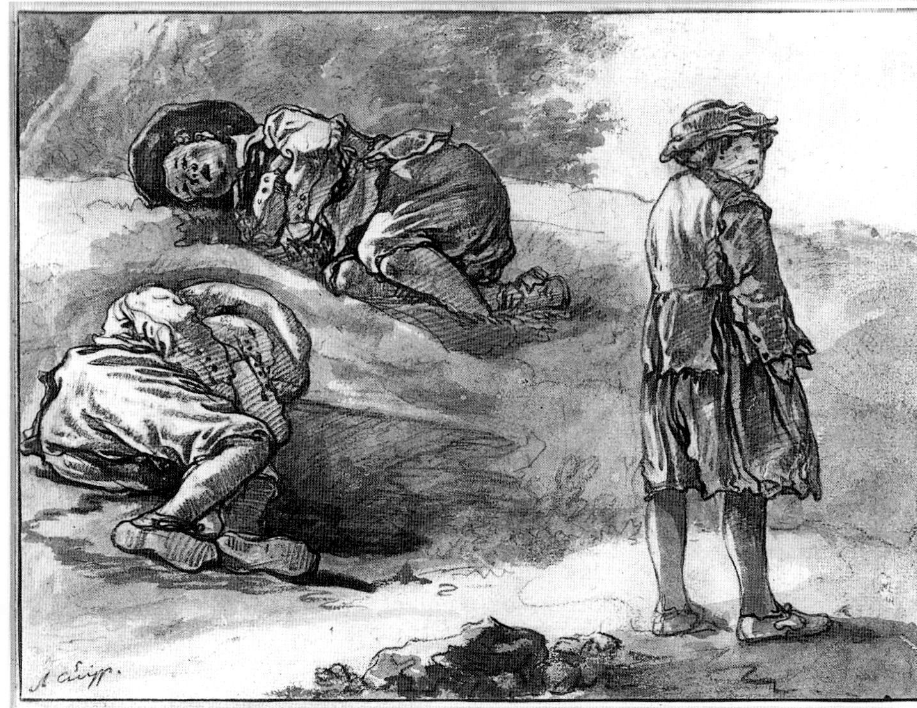

62

Aelbert Cuyp, *Three studies of a shepherd boy.*
Black chalk, grey wash, 147 x 191 mm.
Rijksmuseum, Amsterdam

accents for eyes and eyebrows – a little more subtle but ultimately also more stereotypical than his master. In the landscape in this painting, he is following Jan Both rather than Aelbert Cuyp.

This makes one suspect that Cuyp himself contributed to the confusion by putting assistants to work on important commissions – assistants who, like Van Calraet, then went on to produce their own oeuvres under their own names. But there are also other traps for unwary connoisseurs of Cuyp's work. An 18th-century draughtsman, for instance, added cloudy skies to numerous panoramas by Cuyp (for example figs. 16, 19, 36). The superb drawing of three boys (fig. 62) in the Rijksmuseum is in fact a sheet of studies, in which a sleeping boy was sketched from two angles. A later 'connoisseur' probably wanted to make it into a single entity by putting it into a landscape setting. It might have been worse: sheets like this were not infrequently cut up and sold as individual studies.

The great popularity that Cuyp's work enjoyed in 18th-century England inspired a number of Dutch artists of the day in a variety of ways. More than a few forgeries will have been slipped in among the numerous Cuyps that crossed the North Sea. Countless copies were also made, without a proper record of who the actual artist was, and were then transmogrified into 'genuine Cuyps'. Around 1800, when the Dutch 'rediscovered' their 17th-century golden age, the artists of Dordrecht again came under the spell of Aelbert Cuyp. It was the brothers Abraham and Jacob van Strij who were most assiduous in imitating their 17th-century predecessor. In their turn,

45

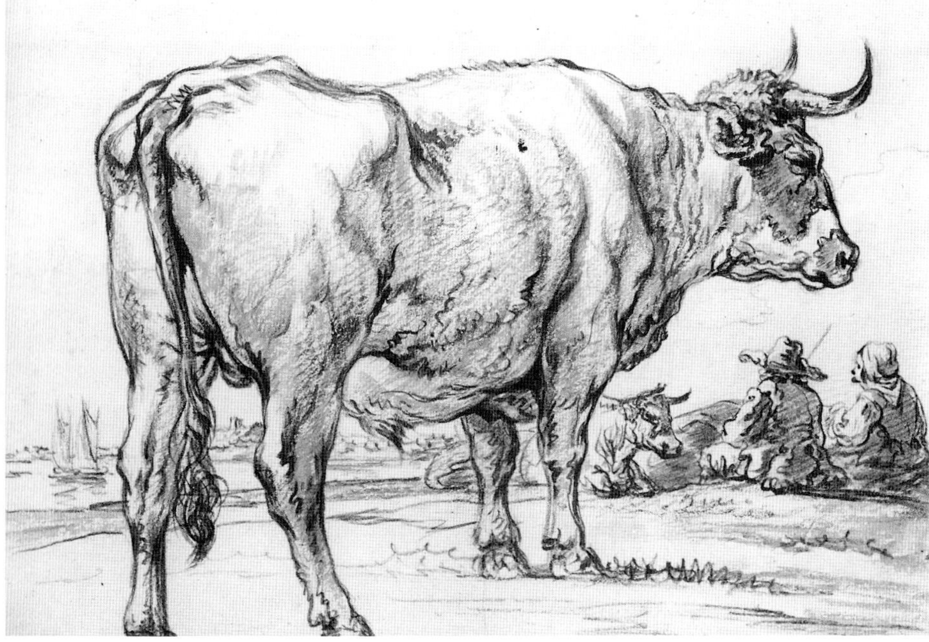

63

Attributed to Jacob van Strij, *A bull.*
Black chalk, grey wash, 197 x 287 mm.
Staatliche Museen zu Berlin-Preussischer Kulturbesitz,
Kupferstichkabinett, Berlin

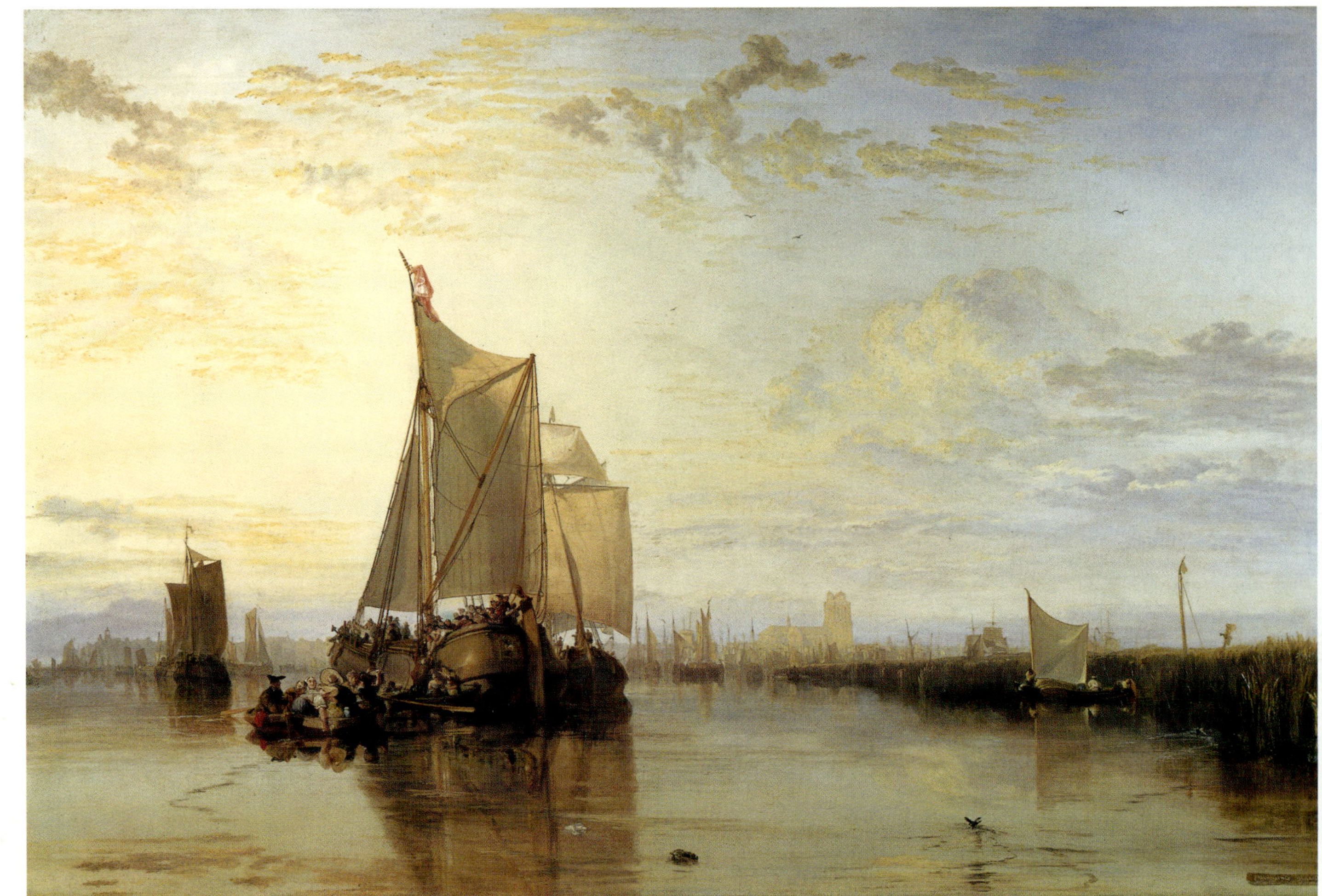

64

J.M.W. Turner, *The Dort packet-boat*

from Rotterdam becalmed, 1818.

Canvas, 157.5 x 233.5 cm.

Yale Center for British Art, New Haven

(Paul Mellon Collection)

drawings by Jacob van Strij (1756-1815) were taken to be works by Cuyp. A good example is *A bull* (fig. 63), a drawing of a subject that is very much Cuyp's province but in which the hand is much more nervous, with swelling lines that Cuyp never used. Some of Van Strij's paintings are real Cuyp imitations, well-intentioned efforts to make a comparable work in Cuyp's style, as in the *Landscape with cattle drover and shep-*

herd (fig. 61), in which the subject, the evening mood and the local use of strong colour are all derived from Cuyp. Happily, Jacob van Strij also produced some splendid work in which he gave an entirely individual direction to the inspiration he drew from Cuyp.

FAME AND LACK OF APPRECIATION

Cuyp enjoyed great fame abroad, particularly in England. Substantial sums were paid for his work, and in the Netherlands the owners were so delighted to collect the large amounts they could get for a painting by the master that by the late 19th century there was virtually no work of significance left in Cuyp's own country. Admittedly, there was also immense interest abroad in other great masters of the 17th century, but in no other case did it lead to such a wholesale sell-out.

Cuyp's renown is also evident from the inspiration that innumerable artists drew from his work. Cuyp was known in England as 'the Dutch Claude', and this tells us straight away why he was valued: for the peaceful atmosphere, for the golden glow, for his own Dutch look compared with the French exemplar, whose scenes are always set in an idealized Antiquity. But Cuyp's own style was also respected. Constable, for instance, acknowledged the qualities of the contrast between light and shade in Cuyp's paintings. Turner (1775-1851) appreciated above all the ambiance of ships in calm weather, as in *The Maas at Dordrecht* (fig. 42). When he visited Holland in 1817, he went to Dordrecht, where his thoughts must have turned frequently to Cuyp. His masterly *The Dort packet-boat from Rotterdam becalmed* of 1818 (fig. 64) is a veritable ode to Aelbert Cuyp as a painter of Dordrecht and the water.

The French, too, held Cuyp in considerable admiration, as we can see from this paean by Marcel Proust (1871-1922), which was written in 1896.

Cuyp, soleil déclinant dissous, dans l'air limpide

Cuyp, setting sun dissolves in the limpid air that

Qu'un vol de ramiers gris trouble comme l'eau,

A flight of grey woodpigeons ruffles like water,

Moiteur d'or, nimbe au front d'un boeuf ou d'un bouleau,

Golden haze, nimbus on the brow of a bull or a birch,

Encens bleu des beaux jours fumant sur le coteau,

Blue incense of fine days smoking on the hillside,

Ou marais de clarté stagnant dans le ciel vide.

Or a clear marsh, motionless under the empty sky.

Des cavaliers sont prêts, plume rose au chapeau,

The horsemen are ready, pink feather in hat,

Paume au coté; l'air vif qui fait rose leur peau,

Hand on hip; the keen air reddens their skin,

Enfle légèrement leurs fines boucles blondes,

Gently stirs their handsome golden curls,

Et, tentés par les champs ardents, les fraîches ondes,

And seduced by the glowing fields, the cooling waves,

Sans troubler par leur trot les boeufs dont le troupeau

Their hoof beats not troubling the cattle as the herd

Rêve dans un brouillard d'or pâle et de repos,

Dreams peacefully in a mist of pale gold,

Ils partent respirer ces minutes profondes.

They set out, breathing in these intense moments.

Proust has precisely captured the dignified
peace that is so characteristic of Cuyp's
paintings. The fact that he was looking
at a painting in the Louvre in Paris that is
now regarded as a studio piece does not
detract from this in any way. Proust's friend
Reynaldo Hahn composed an etude for
piano based on this poem – the direction
'très calme' is almost self-evident.

In the Netherlands, Cuyp's work continued to be undervalued. It took a very
long time before Dutch museums were
prepared to fork out the enormous sums
that were paid for Cuyp's work in other
countries. Although the impressive *Maas
at Dordrecht* (fig. 42) came up for sale in the
nineteen-twenties and the lack of a Cuyp
in the Netherlands was already keenly felt,
the then director of the Rijksmuseum,
F. Schmidt Degener, made no attempt to
acquire the painting for the Netherlands.
Schmidt Degener, who had very decided
tastes when it came to Dutch art, men-
tions Cuyp only in passing in his essay
'The Enduring Image of Dutch Art', while
elsewhere he refers to him as one of the
'grand seigneurs' of that same art. This latter epithet reflects respect, but no love. He
probably saw the Arcadian atmosphere of
Cuyp's landscapes and the warm sunlight
as being un-Dutch.

Around 1950 the situation had in fact
changed very little – the balance had still
not tipped in Cuyp's favour. Two purchases
of work by Cuyp made for the Rijksmuseum
in the nineteen-fifties seem to have been
prompted by parsimony rather than by
any desire to represent the master with a
work of stature. It was not until 1965, with
the acquisition of the *River landscape with
two horsemen* (fig. 52), that a major Cuyp was
purchased for a Dutch museum. It was only
then that Aelbert Cuyp received the recog-
nition in his own country that had long
been his elsewhere.

ACKNOWLEDGEMENTS

The main publications on Aelbert Cuyp
and his oeuvre on which I drew when
writing this *Dossier* are:
-   Stephen Reiss, *Aelbert Cuyp*, London 1975
-   J.M. de Groot et al., *Aelbert Cuyp en zijn
    familie, schilders te Dordrecht*, Dordrecht
    (Dordrechts Museum) 1978
-   Alan Chong, *Aelbert Cuyp and the Meanings
    of Landscape*, Ann Arbor (diss. New York
    University) 1992
-   Arthur K. Wheelock Jr. (ed.), *Aelbert Cuyp*,
    Washington (National Gallery of Art),
    London (National Gallery), Amsterdam
    (Rijksmuseum) 2001-2002, with intro-
    ductory essays by Arthur K. Wheelock,
    Alan Chong, Emilie Gordenker, Marika
    Spring, Egbert Haverkamp-Begemann,
    and with descriptions of the works by
    Alan Chong, Axel Rüger, Arthur K.
    Wheelock and Wouter Kloek.

I am greatly indebted to Egbert Haverkamp-
Begemann, who initiated me into Aelbert
Cuyp's oeuvre of drawings and persuaded
me of Cuyp's precocious talent as a draughtsman. He also gave me access to the
numerous findings of Jan G. van Gelder
and Ingrid Jost, whose proposed mono-
graph on the drawings of Aelbert Cuyp
he will be completing.

I should like to thank Fieke Tissink,
Erwin Kroll, Sander Paarlberg and Marijn
Schapelhouman for their assistance, and
Ger Luijten and Maud Soethout for their
critical reading of the manuscript.

Dordrecht viewed from the water